PACAF
AND ALASKAN AIR
COMMAND IN THE 1980s

Adrian Symonds

AMBERLEY

Acknowledgements

I would like to thank Sally Tunnicliffe for her assistance. Special thanks go to my wife, Louise, and son, Charlie, for their support and patience.

This book is dedicated to the men and women of the United States Air Force who served in Pacific Air Forces and Alaskan Air Command.

Note on Korean transliteration

In 2002 South Korea replaced the 'McCune–Reischauer' (MR) system, which represented the Korean language when transcribed and transliterated into Latin script, with the new 'Revised Romanization of Korean' (RR) system. Subsequently, many South Korean place names were changed when transliterated into Latin script. For example, the place transliterated into Latin as Taegu under MR is transliterated Daegu under RR; Pusan under MR is transliterated Busan under RR. However, for the purposes of this text, the former MR transliteration system is used, reflecting the transliteration system in use during the time period covered by this title.

First published 2024

Amberley Publishing
The Hill, Stroud
Gloucestershire, GL5 4EP

www.amberley-books.com

Copyright © Adrian Symonds, 2024

The right of Adrian Symonds to be identified as the Author of this work has been asserted in accordance with the Copyrights, Designs and Patents Act 1988.

ISBN 978 1 3981 1584 2 (print)
ISBN 978 1 3981 1585 9 (ebook)

British Library Cataloguing in Publication Data.
A catalogue record for this book is available from the British Library.

Typesetting by SJmagic DESIGN SERVICES, India.
Printed in the UK.

Contents

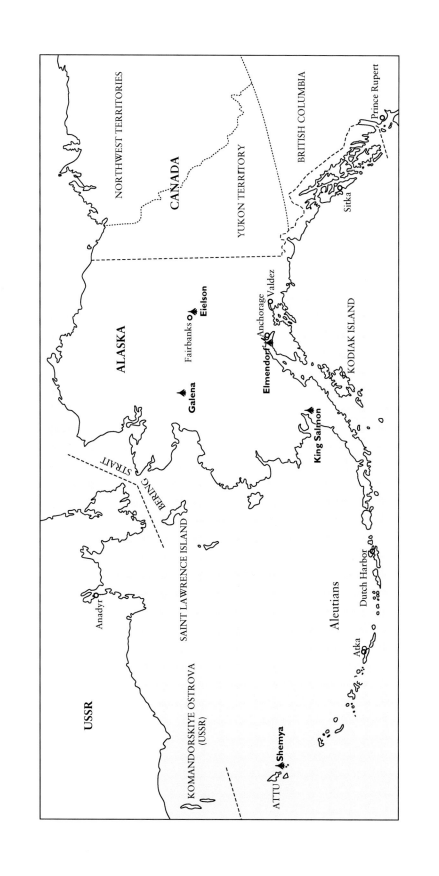

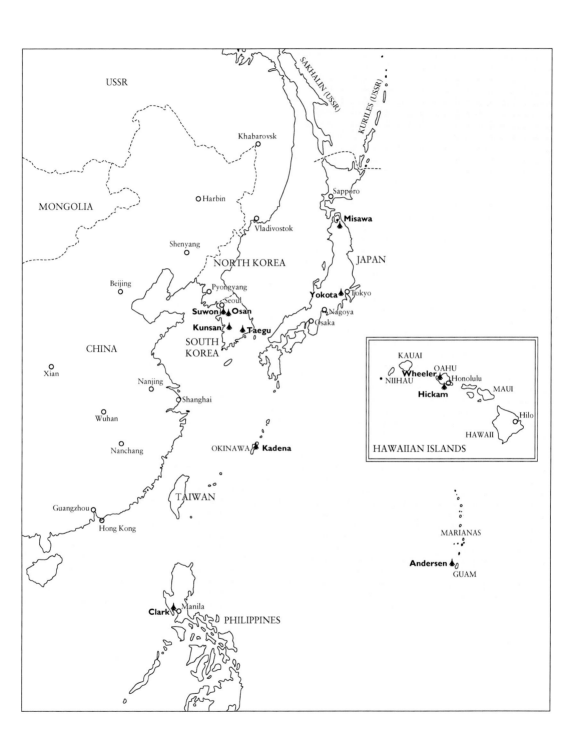

Introduction

Pacific Air Forces (PACAF) is a Major Command (MAJCOM) of the United States Air Force (USAF) headquartered at Hickam Air Force Base (AFB), Oahu, Hawaii (which today is part of Joint Base Pearl Harbor–Hickam). PACAF is one of only two USAF MAJCOMs to be forward-deployed outside the United States.

Despite having responsibility for providing tactical air power throughout the huge Asia-Pacific region, during the last decade of the Cold War PACAF was dwarfed numerically by the USAF's other forward-deployed MAJCOM, which was the United States Air Forces in Europe (USAFE). PACAF was roughly half the size of USAFE, reflecting the Cold War focus on Europe, despite PACAF being responsible for an area of over 100 million square miles, covering the Pacific and Indian Ocean areas, and with forces spread as far apart as Hawaii, Japan, the Republic of Korea (ROK/South Korea) and the Philippines.

PACAF units routinely interacted with allied air arms. Here an F-15C Eagle of the 12th TFS, 18th TFW, leads an F-4E Phantom II and an F-5E Tiger II of the Republic of Korea Air Force (ROKAF), then the primary ROKAF fighter types, as well as an F-4E of the 36th TFS, 51st TFW and nearest the camera the 8th TFW wing commander's F-16A Fighting Falcon (as shown by the colours of both of the wing's squadrons on the fin stripe as well as the '8 TFW' markings). This formation was flown on 15 March 1984 during exercise Team Spirit '84. Team Spirit was an annual tactical exercise that had been conducted in South Korea each spring since 1974; it would continue until 1993. As well as involving South Korean and Korean-based US military units, US units deployed to Korea from elsewhere in the Pacific and the United States, practising their wartime reinforcement duties. (National Archives and Records Administration)

Originally activated as Far East Air Forces (FEAF) on 3 August 1944, it was redesignated Pacific Air Forces on 1 July 1957. FEAF was considerably reinforced by USAF units from the US-based MAJCOMs during the Korean War (1950–53) and likewise PACAF was reinforced during the Vietnam War (with the primary PACAF commitment to combat in South East Asia being from 1964 to 1973). Before being committed to Vietnam, PACAF had reduced to 65,155 personnel and 582 aircraft; during the war in South East Asia, PACAF peaked at 170,000 personnel and 2,100 aircraft. PACAF wound down its involvement in South East Asia from 1970 as the conduct of the war was handed over by the Americans to the South Vietnamese under 'Vietnamization'. PACAF withdrew from South Vietnamese air bases in 1973 and ceased combat operations. PACAF also withdrew from Thai air bases in 1976; by that year PACAF had been reduced to 34,111 personnel and 255 aircraft. The normalisation of US relations with the People's Republic of China (PRC) also saw PACAF withdraw from Ching Chuan Kang Air Base in the Republic of China (Taiwan) in 1979.

When FEAF was redesignated PACAF on 1 July 1957, it was assigned two Numbered Air Forces: Fifth Air Force (5 AF) and Thirteenth Air Force (13 AF). During the period of the Vietnam War, PACAF was assigned an additional Numbered Air Force,

The squadron commander's F-15D and an F-15C of the 67th TFS, 18th TFW lead Royal Australian Air Force (RAAF) Mirages during exercise Pacific Consort in Australia in September 1980. The Mirage IIIO single-seater and Mirage IIID two-seater were from No. 2 Operational Conversion Unit (OCU), the Mirage training unit, at RAAF Base Williamtown, New South Wales. The F-15s retain their 'turkey feather' aerodynamic exhaust petals which covered the nozzles of their Pratt & Whitney F100 afterburning turbofan engines. To reduce maintenance requirements, they were later removed from F-15s, however this increased aerodynamic drag by 3 per cent. The F-15s carry CATM-9Ls while the Mirages carry CATM-9Bs, inert captive training variants of the AIM-9 Sidewinder short-range air-to-air missile (AAM), featuring a working seeker, but lacking a live warhead or rocket motor. (NARA)

Seventh Air Force (7 AF), which was activated on 28 March 1966. As PACAF forces wound down after the Vietnam War, 7 AF inactivated on 30 June 1975.

Therefore, as the 1980s dawned, PACAF was assigned Fifth Air Force, which was responsible for units stationed in Japan and South Korea, and Thirteenth Air Force, which was responsible for units stationed in the Philippines.

However, on 8 September 1986 PACAF returned to being assigned three Numbered Air Forces when Seventh Air Force was reactivated, taking over responsibility for units in South Korea from Fifth Air Force, the latter henceforth focussing solely on Japan.

By 1989 PACAF had 38,860 personnel (28,856 military and 10,004 civilian) and around 300 combat aircraft. It is notable that some PACAF wings adopted non-standard organisational structures when compared with the wing structures of the other tactical USAF MAJCOMs (TAC (Tactical Air Command) and USAFE) at that time. This included wings with intermediate groups between the wing headquarters and the flying squadrons, and wings with one or more of their assigned flying squadrons operating as geographically separated units (GSUs), based away from the wing headquarters.

Alaskan Air Command (AAC), headquartered at Elmendorf AFB, Alaska, was also a MAJCOM, and was responsible for conducting air operations within the state of Alaska.

Mainland Alaska was separated from the mainland Union of Soviet Socialist Republics (USSR – Soviet Union) by just 50 miles across the Bering Strait, therefore AAC had vital Cold War responsibilities. This included providing air-defence aircraft and air-defence radar systems. While these were administratively controlled by AAC they were operationally controlled in their air-defence duties by the binational US-Canadian North American Air Defense Command (NORAD, redesignated the North American Aerospace Defense Command in March 1981).

AAC was one of the smallest USAF MAJCOMs; by 1989 AAC had 8,790 personnel (7,512 military and 1,278 civilian). By measure of personnel on strength, as of 1989 the only smaller USAF MAJCOMs were the Air University (7,339 total military and civilian personnel) and Air Force Space Command (7,922 total military and civilian personnel). Therefore, on 9 August 1990, as the Soviet threat began to reduce and the Cold War neared its end, AAC was redesignated Eleventh Air Force (11 AF) and changed its status from a USAF MAJCOM to a Numbered Air Force subordinate to PACAF.

Both PACAF and AAC were expanded and modernised during the 1980s, as part of the wider expansion and modernisation of the US armed forces during the decade.

As with previous books in this series, space dictates that primarily only flying units are covered within this title. However, there were (as for all USAF commands) many non-flying units throughout PACAF and AAC. The majority of personnel would have served in non-flying units, such as Special Security, Civil Engineering, Air Postal, School, Computer Services, Field Printing, Management Engineering and Materiel Squadrons. Within the various wings detailed, as well as flying squadrons, supporting units included Aircraft Generation, Component Repair and Equipment Maintenance Squadrons. There was also the wing-command post plus offices and units for intelligence, weapons and tactics, plans and standardisation-evaluation ('stan/eval').

As was the case with USAFE in Europe (see this author's *USAFE in the 1980s*), PACAF in the Asia-Pacific region and AAC in Alaska both required the support of flying and non-flying units from the various commands based in the contiguous

A 12th TFS, 18th TFW F-15C leads Japan Air Self-Defense Force (JASDF) Mitsubishi F-1s during exercise Cope North 85-1. The F-1s are from the JASDF's 3 Hikotai, 3 Kokudan (3rd Squadron, 3rd Air Wing), based at Misawa AB under the JASDF's Hokubu Koku Homentai (Northern Air Defence Command). (NARA)

United States. These units were permanently, rotationally or temporarily deployed to the respective areas of responsibility of PACAF and AAC. Such support came from Strategic Air Command (SAC), Military Airlift Command (MAC), Tactical Air Command (TAC), Air National Guard (ANG), Air Force Reserve (AFRES), Air Force Communications Command (AFCC), Electronic Security Command (ESC) and Space Command (SPACECOM).

The Threat

Naturally, as part of the global Cold War, the primary threat faced by the United States and her allies throughout the region during the 1980s was that presented by the colossal forces of the Soviet Union. Meanwhile, the large regional forces of the Democratic People's Republic of Korea (DPRK – North Korea) required constant vigilance in the defence of South Korea. Vietnam was no longer a particular focus for US forces, although Soviet aircraft were stationed there during the 1980s.

Sino-Soviet relations had soured during the 1960s to the extent that the People's Republic of China and the Soviet Union (hitherto the two leading communist powers, in an alliance set upon world revolution) fought a border conflict; this was seized upon by the United States, which set out to improve relations with the PRC from 1969 onwards in order to isolate and pressure the Soviet Union as part of the United States' Cold War strategy. Consequently, President Richard Nixon, under the Nixon Doctrine, proclaimed his intentions to reduce US military commitments in Asia and to reconsider the policy of containment for the PRC. During the 1970s Sino-US relations were slowly normalised, one consequence of which, as noted above, was that remaining US forces withdrew from Taiwan, which China viewed as a rogue province. However, the Taiwan Relations Act, signed by President Carter in 1979, committed the United States to provide military and other support for Taiwan. Consequently, Chinese forces remained a potential threat, especially if they had attacked Taiwan.

Pacific Air Forces

Fifth Air Force

During the 1980s Fifth Air Force (5 AF), headquartered at Yokota Air Base (AB), Japan, was initially responsible for PACAF's air operations in Japan and South Korea. Later, on 8 September 1986, the Korean-based elements of Fifth Air Force (which were under 314th Air Division) were reassigned from Fifth Air Force to the newly reactivated Seventh Air Force, subsequently leaving Fifth Air Force with just the Japanese-based elements.

Fifth Air Force's 313th Air Division (AD) at Kadena AB, Okinawa, Japan, controlled the 18th Tactical Fighter Wing (TFW), which was assigned the 'ZZ' tail code and was also stationed at Kadena AB. From 1 May 1978 there was an intermediate 18th Tactical Fighter Group (TFG) between the 18th TFW and its flying squadrons. Assigned to the 18th TFG at the start of the decade were the following: 1st Special Operations Squadron (SOS) (no tail code or squadron colour), the 15th Tactical Reconnaissance Squadron (TRS) 'No-Gun Shoguns' (black/yellow checkerboard fin stripe), 12th Tactical Fighter Squadron (TFS) 'Bald Eagles' (yellow fin stripe), 25th TFS 'Assam Dragons' (green fin stripe), 44th TFS 'Vampires' (black fin stripe), and 67th TFS 'Fighting Cocks' (red fin stripe). The wing also maintained Det 1, 18th TFW, which was forward-deployed at Osan AB, South Korea. The 18th TFG inactivated on 11 February 1981, and subsequently the squadrons were assigned directly to 18th TFW.

The 1st SOS operated the MC-130E Combat Talon I, in the MC-130E-Y (Yank) sub-variant; the 'Yank' was equipped with a standard 'Pinocchio' nose radome and lacked the Fulton surface-to-air recovery system (STARS) gear and chin radome of the MC-130E-C (Clamp) sub-variant used by the TAC and USAFE special operations squadrons.

MC-130Es were required for Operation Eagle Claw, the 1980 attempt to rescue US hostages from Iran. Fourteen MC-130Es were in USAF service when planning for the operation began in 1979; four 'Yanks' with PACAF's 1st SOS at Kadena AB, four 'Clamps' with USAFE's 7th SOS at Rhein-Main AB, West Germany, and six 'Clamps' with TAC's 8th SOS at Hurlburt Field, Florida. However, only seven of these fourteen USAF MC-130Es had at that time been modified for in-flight refuelling (IFR); the IFR-modified aircraft were all four of the 1st SOS MC-130E 'Yanks' and three of the six 8th SOS MC-130E 'Clamps'. Therefore, with IFR being essential to the operation, the 1st SOS was heavily involved in the preparation and conduct of the operation, in conjunction with TAC's 8th SOS. New NVG (night vision goggle) blacked-out landing procedures and in-flight refuelling procedures were developed jointly by PACAF's 1st SOS and TAC's 8th SOS, which practised night refuelling from SAC KC-135As.

Eventually, it was decided that three MC-130Es would fly in the 118-man Delta Force assault team, plus Rangers to provide security, from Masirah Island, Oman, to the 'Desert One' forward staging area in the Iranian desert during the hours of darkness. They would be joined there by three EC-130Es (from TAC's 7th ACCS, but flown by 8th SOS crews), the latter acting as ground tankers with bladder fuel tanks in the hold in place of their usual removable AN/ASC-15 command battle staff module. The three MC-130Es were 8th SOS 'Clamp' airframes; however, two of their three crews came from the 1st SOS. Meanwhile, a spare MC-130E was held on standby; this was a 1st SOS 'Yank' aircraft with a 1st SOS crew. The MC/EC-130s would be met at 'Desert One' by eight RH-53D helicopters (from US Navy squadron HM-16) flying in from the USS *Nimitz*. The RH-53Ds would refuel on the ground from the EC-130Es and load the Delta Force personnel, which the MC-130Es had brought in. They would then move the rescue force to 'Desert Two', a hide site nearer to Tehran, from where the rescue operation would proceed overland.

When Operation Eagle Claw was launched on 24 April 1980, of the eight RH-53Ds that had launched, only six successfully arrived at 'Desert One'; a short time later one of the remaining RH-53Ds collided with an EC-130E at 'Desert One', tragically killing three crew aboard the RH-53D and five aboard the EC-130E. With only five RH-53Ds remaining, this brought the number below the minimum (six) required to proceed, and the operation was aborted. The remaining helicopters were abandoned and there was a scramble as all surviving personnel boarded the remaining MC-130E (the two others having by that time already taken off again to return to Masirah Island) and two surviving EC-130Es for evacuation. (For more details of the operation, see this author's *US Naval Aviation in the 1980s: Air Stations of the Atlantic and Pacific Fleets*.)

On 1 January 1981 the 1st SOS moved – formally termed a 'permanent change of station' (PCS) – to Clark AB in the Philippines; on 15 January 1981 1st SOS was reassigned from 18th TFG to Clark's 3d TFW (q.v.).

The 15th TRS operated RF-4Cs; when 18th TFG inactivated on 11 February 1981 15th TRS was reassigned directly to 18th TFW. During the 1980s the 15th TRS's RF-4Cs received the AN/ARN-101 Digital Modular Avionics System (DMAS) digital avionics upgrade, greatly improving their performance; this is described in more detail below. On 1 October 1989 the 460th Tactical Reconnaissance Group (TRG) was activated at Taegu AB, South Korea, under Seventh Air Force; on that date 15th TRS moved from Kadena to Taegu and was reassigned from 18th TFW to 460th TRG, replacing the 'ZZ' tail code with 'GU'.

The 12th TFS and 25th TFS both operated F-4Ds at the start of 1980, while the 44th TFS and 67th TFS operated F-15C/Ds, having transitioned from F-4Ds on 1 January 1980 and 1 October 1979 respectively. The 12th TFS subsequently transitioned to the F-15C/D on 1 April 1980. The 25th TFS, therefore, became the final Kadena F-4D squadron and was the only Kadena F-4D squadron not to transition to the F-15; although it was not inactivated, 25th TFS was reduced to zero strength and became non-operational from 22 August 1980. Although inactive, the 25th TFS remained assigned to the 18th TFG 'on paper' until 1 February 1981; on that date the 25th TFS was moved without personnel or equipment (i.e. an administrative 'paper' reassignment) to Suwon AB, South Korea, and reassigned to the 51st Composite Wing (Tactical), finally receiving A-10As from January 1982 (q.v.).

The 18th TFW's three F-15C/D squadrons undertook their training with TAC's 33d TFW at Eglin AFB, Florida, before returning to Kadena. During this early phase of

A 15th TRS, 18th TFW RF-4C over Korea while operating from Osan AB during Team Spirit '82 in March 1982. The 'lump' on the spine is the main recognition feature that shows that this RF-4C, like all 15th TRS jets, has received the AN/ARN-101 Digital Modular Avionics System (DMAS) digital avionics upgrade. (NARA)

Ground crew wearing nuclear, biological and chemical (NBC) 'Mission Oriented Protective Posture' (MOPP) suits preparing a 15th TRS RF-4C for flight at Osan during Team Spirit '86 in March 1986. The RF-4C carries an AN/ALQ-119 (long version) electronic countermeasures (ECM) pod under the port wing. PACAF retained AN/ALQ-119 during the 1980s, while USAFE switched to the new AN/ALQ-131 pod. (NARA)

A 15th TRS RF-4C streaming its drag chute while landing at Osan during Team Spirit '85 in March 1985. It displays the wraparound version of the South East Asia (SEA) camouflage scheme, consisting of FS 34102 medium green, FS 34079 dark green and FS 30219 dark tan with toned-down national insignia. The original SEA scheme had included FS 36622 light-grey undersides and full-colour national insignia. (NARA)

Four 15th TRS RF-4Cs in flight near Kadena AB on 14 January 1988. They are finished in the F-4 variant of the USAF's 'European I' wraparound camouflage, which had replaced the SEA scheme from the mid-1980s. This retained the dark green and medium green used in the 'SEA' scheme, but replaced the former dark tan with FS 36081 dark grey. (NARA)

A 15th TRS RF-4E takes off from Misawa on 15 December 1988 during exercise Orient Shield, part of exercise Cope North 89-1. By now the two-tone medium grey (FS 26270) and dark grey (FS 26118) 'Hill Gray II' camouflage scheme was replacing 'European I'. (NARA)

USAF F-15 operations, the 33d TFW at Eglin, although a combat-coded front-line wing, was assisting other units in their transition to the F-15, both with training and airframes. It had originally been equipped with F-15A/Bs, but transitioned to F-15C/Ds during 1979/80 (passing its F-15A/Bs on to the 49th TFW at Holloman AFB, New Mexico). The 33d TFW then used its new F-15C/Ds to train the Kadena/18th TFW personnel (including fifty-five pilots). The 33d TFW progressively transferred its fifty-four F-15C/Ds to the 18th TFW's three F-15C/D squadrons under 'Ready Eagle III'. This gave a unit establishment of eighteen aircraft per squadron, lower than the more usual twenty-four aircraft per squadron. The first stage of Ready Eagle III saw eighteen F-15C/Ds move from Eglin to Kadena on 26 September 1979 to equip the 67th TFS; Ready Eagle III was completed on 16 April 1980 when the final F-15C/Ds arrived at Kadena to complete the re-equipment of the 12th TFS. Meanwhile, the 33d TFW at Eglin reverted to F-15A/Bs, receiving ex-USAFE 36th TFW airframes from Bitburg AB, West Germany.

Personnel from the 8th TFW's 8th Component Repair Squadron prepare an icy 12th TFS F-15C at Kwang Ju AB on 1 March 1981 during Team Spirit '81. Kwang Ju was an active-duty USAF base 150 miles south of Seoul; it had no permanently based flying units and was intended to support forward-deployed USAF flying units in wartime. In peacetime it was regularly used by ROKAF and USAF units. The base was handed over to the Republic of Korea in 1991. (NARA)

Two 12th TFS F-15Cs being refuelled from fuel bladder pits at Kwang Ju during Team Spirit '81. The nearest aircraft carries a CATM-9L captive training Sidewinder. The aircraft both feature the original simple single-colour tail stripe, yellow in the case of the 12th TFS. (NARA)

A 12th TFS F-15C taking off from Kadena on 18 October 1984, viewed from the back seat of an F-15D. The F-15D carries a practice CATM-9L/M under the wing. MAC C-141Bs can be seen in the background. (NARA)

Left to right: Airman First Class James R. Nichols, Sergeant Ricky Brown and Senior Airman Victor Allen carry a CATM-9L/M training Sidewinder away from a 12th TFS F-15C while deployed to Kwang Ju during Team Spirit '84. The men are aircraft armament specialists with the 18th TFW's 18th Aircraft Generation Squadron. (NARA)

A spread formation of four 12th TFS F-15Cs in flight on 15 February 1984, carrying centreline 600 US gallon fuel tanks. (NARA)

Three 12th TFS F-15Cs in flight near Kadena on 14 January 1988. The foreground aircraft displays the 'Mod Eagle' camouflage scheme that was at that time being introduced by the 18th TFW to replace the 'Ghost Gray' scheme used hitherto, as seen on the other jets. 'Ghost Gray' consisted of FS 36375 light grey and FS 36320 dark grey; Mod Eagle consisted of FS 36251 light grey and FS 37176 dark grey. Although initially introduced by PACAF, Mod Eagle later replaced 'Ghost Gray' on all USAF F-15A/B/C/Ds. (NARA)

Air Marshal John 'Jake' Newham, RAAF Chief of the Air Staff, examining the cockpit of a 44th TFS F-15C deployed to RAAF Williamtown during exercise Coral Sea '85. Air Marshal Newham is looking into a rifle 'scope fitted to the heads-up display (HUD). In scenarios requiring visual identification (VID) of targets, use of AIM-7F Sparrow medium-range AAM was precluded as there was no means to VID targets before the minimum AIM-7F range was reached. As a makeshift solution to this problem the 'Eagle Eye' was born; Bushnell nine-power hunting rifle 'scopes bolted to the HUD, boresighted with the HUD centre. The pilot centred the hostile target in the HUD and looked down the scope to VID the target beyond minimum AIM-7F range. It was workable, but better in theory than practice. A longer-term solution was Non Cooperative Target Recognition (NCTR, pronounced 'nectar'), which analysed the target's engine compressor and turbine blade radar returns to identify the type that the F-15's AN/APG-63 radar was 'painting'. NCTR was introduced, along with many other improvements under the Multi-Stage Improvement Program (MSIP) that Eagles were put through in the mid to late 1980s. (NARA)

A welcoming ceremony for 18th TFW personnel arriving at Kwang Ju for Team Spirit '85 on 1 March 1985, with 44th TFS F-15Cs in the background. (NARA)

Three 44th TFS F-15Cs in formation during Team Spirit '85, carrying centreline fuel tanks. The far aircraft carries an CATM-9L/M; the other two aircraft are likely to be similarly equipped. (NARA)

Maintenance personnel and pilots pre-flight 44th TFS F-15s deployed to Andersen AFB, Guam, during exercise Giant Warrior '89 on 27 March 1989. The third aircraft from the front is an F-15D, the rest F-15Cs. The third F-15C from the rear is in the Mod Eagle scheme, the others retaining 'Ghost Gray'. By this time the 18th TFW's squadrons had returned to a single squadron colour stripe, here black for the 44th TFS. A 60th BMS B-52G is in the background. (NARA)

When the three squadrons transitioned from F-4Ds to F-15C/Ds, they initially retained the conventional squadron tail-stripe markings with a single colour: 12th TFS yellow, 44th TFS black (having used blue on its F-4s) and 67th TFS red. However, each later adopted a triangular fin flash involving all three colours, with the prominent outermost colour being the actual squadron colour (each retaining the same squadron colour as before). Late in the decade the squadrons began to revert to the single-colour tail stripe.

Det 1, 18th TFW-controlled F-15C/Ds and RF-4Cs forward-deployed by the wing from Kadena to Osan AB. The 18th TFW's three F-15 squadrons contributed aircraft and crews to Osan AB under Det 1. Det 1's temporary duty (TDY) F-15s at Osan provided twenty-four-hour air-defence alert, greatly augmenting the air-defence-tasked USAF F-4s and F-16s and Republic of Korea Air Force (ROKAF) F-4s and F-5s (and later F-16s) permanently based in Korea. Meanwhile, to be nearer to their likely wartime operating area the 15th TRS maintained a permanent seven- or eight-aircraft RF-4C forward detachment at Osan AB under Det 1. The primary peacetime role of the forward-deployed RF-4Cs was to keep an eye on the Korean Demilitarized Zone (DMZ) with their cameras and infra-red linescan equipment, which they could accomplish from South Korean airspace. Personnel were rotated every few weeks from Kadena to Osan to support Det 1.

Seen during exercise Ostfriesland II on 9 February 1983, two 67th TFS F-15Cs and a 15th TRS RF-4C overfly the Soviet aircraft carrier *Minsk* (officially rated by the Soviets as a Heavy Aircraft-Carrying Cruiser) as it sailed in the Pacific. (NARA)

A 67th TFS F-15C pilot discusses a possible maintenance problem with ground crewmen during the joint JASDF and PACAF Cope North '84-1 at Chitose AB, Japan, on 10 October 1983. Exercises were named for the fiscal year in which they fell, rather than the calendar year; fiscal year 1984 commenced on 1 October 1983. (NARA)

Two 67th TFS F-15Cs in flight on 18 October 1983 during Cope North '84-1. The far aircraft retains the single red tail stripe while the near aircraft has the newer multi-coloured triangular fin flash with the outer colour being the actual squadron colour. Both F-15Cs carry centreline fuel tanks. The far aircraft carries a CATM-9L/M under the port wing; the near aircraft carries one out of sight under the starboard wing. (NARA)

As noted above, the 15th TRS, 12th TFS, 44th TFS and 67th TFS were assigned directly to 18th TFW after the intermediate 18th TFG was inactivated on 11 February 1981.

The 3d TFW's 26th Aggressor Squadron at Clark AB in the Philippines was reassigned to the 18th TFW and moved to Kadena without aircraft on 1 October

The 67th TFS F-15Cs seen in the previous image during the same mission. (NARA)

A 67th TFS F-15C in flight on 15 February 1984, the 'turkey feather' aerodynamic exhaust petals by now removed from the F100 engine nozzles. (NARA)

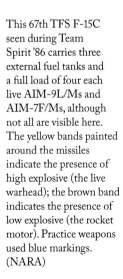

This 67th TFS F-15C seen during Team Spirit '86 carries three external fuel tanks and a full load of four each live AIM-9L/Ms and AIM-7F/Ms, although not all are visible here. The yellow bands painted around the missiles indicate the presence of high explosive (the live warhead); the brown band indicates the presence of low explosive (the rocket motor). Practice weapons used blue markings. (NARA)

Ground crewmen perform maintenance on 67th TFS F-15Cs deployed to Clark AB during exercise Cope Thunder '89-5. The 18th TFW's squadrons had by then returned to a single squadron colour stripe. (NARA)

A Flight Systems Sabre is prepared for a mission. Three civilian-registered, 1954-vintage, ex-Royal Canadian Air Force Canadair CL-13 Sabre Mk 5s were operated from Kadena under contract by Flight Systems Incorporated of Mojave, California, from June 1982 onwards, supporting PACAF with aerial gunnery target towing. They were flown by three former USAF fighter 'jocks' and supported by five maintenance men. Although based at Kadena, they periodically deployed to other PACAF air bases, including Misawa, Osan and Taegu. (NARA)

1988, ahead of a planned transition to the F-16C Block 30 (having operated F-5Es at Clark). However, as described below in the Thirteenth Air Force section, these plans were soon dropped and the 26th AS later inactivated on 21 February 1990 without having become operational with F-16s.

An A/A37U-15 Target Tow System (TTS) under the port wing of a Flight Systems Sabre, balanced by a standard drop tank under the starboard wing. The A/A37U-15 comprised an RMU-10/A tow reel pod and a TDU-10/B towed aerial gunnery target 'dart'. The 16-foot-long dart was reeled out 2,300 feet (700 metres) behind the Sabre. Scoring was accomplished by counting the bullet holes in the dart, which was subsequently recovered, different aircraft using gun rounds dipped in different-coloured paint to show the scores for each firing aircraft. The dart was equipped with a radar reflector, permitting the use of radar gunsights. It was also retained by the USAF, which generally used F-4s to tow them by the 1980s. However, in USAF use it was being replaced by the far more modern A/A37U-33 and A/A37U-36, which utilised acoustic scoring and real-time RF scoring respectively; 18th TFW F-15s could be equipped with these. (NARA)

Kadena AB also hosted Naval Air Facility (NAF) Kadena, which primarily supported routine US Navy (USN) P-3C deployments as well as other transient naval aircraft.

The 18th TFW was directly assigned CT-39A operational support airlift (OSA) aircraft until 1 October 1984 when they were absorbed by MAC's Det 2, 1403d Military Airlift Squadron (q.v.).

The 314th AD at Osan AB, South Korea, controlled the 8th TFW at Kunsan AB, South Korea, and 51st Composite Wing (Tactical) (COMPW) at Osan AB. While generally speaking PACAF did not always enjoy the same level of priority as USAFE did, the PACAF units based in Korea were high priority due to the immediate threat that the Republic of Korea faced from the forces of North Korea. Consequently, Korean-based units were prioritised within PACAF for new equipment. Although Kunsan was a USAF air base, it also hosted a ROKAF F-4D squadron, the 110th TFS, which was detached from the ROKAF's 11th TFW at Taegu.

The 8th TFW ('WP' tail code, for Wolf Pack, the wing's nickname) at Kunsan AB was assigned the 35th TFS 'Pantons' (blue), 80th TFS 'Juvats' (yellow) and 497th TFS 'Night Owls' (red), all operating F-4Ds; the 497th TFS was a geographically separated unit (GSU) located at Taegu AB, South Korea. The 8th TFW was tasked with air defence, conventional attack and nuclear strike. If the North Koreans had invaded South Korea, the wing would have likely been heavily committed interdicting hostile ground forces and striking enemy airfields.

The 35th TFS transitioned from the F-4D to the F-16A/B Block 10 from 15 September 1981, upgrading to the F-16A/B Block 15 during 1982.

The 80th TFS transitioned from the F-4D to a mixed fleet of F-16A/B Block 10s and 15s during the period January–March 1982.

The 497th TFS had only been activated on 1 October 1978, located separately to the rest of the wing as a GSU at Taegu AB; most of its F-4Ds had come from Kadena as the 18th TFW traded its F-4Ds for F-15C/Ds. Taegu was a ROKAF air base, home to the ROKAF's F-4D-equipped 11th TFW. On 1 January 1982 the 497th TFS was reassigned from 8th TFW to 51st COMPW, although remaining stationed at Taegu. This subsequently left the 8th TFW with two flying squadrons.

At the start of the 1980s the 51st COMPW ('OS' tail code) at Osan AB was assigned the 36th TFS 'Flying Fiends' (red) and 19th Tactical Air Support Squadron, Light (TASS) (no squadron colour). The 36th TFS operated F-4Es, primarily in the air-to-air role. The 19th TASS operated forward air control (FAC) OV-10As, and also maintained a detachment, 19th TASS Detachment 1, at Camp Casey, South Korea.

A 35th TFS, 8th TFW F-4D taking off. It features the original SEA camouflage scheme with light-grey undersides and full-colour national insignia. (NARA)

Two 35th TFS F-16A Block 10s during Team Spirit '82, in the original F-16 'Egyptian I' camouflage scheme of FS 36270 medium-grey/ FS 36118 Gunship Gray upper sides with FS 36375 light-grey undersides. Identifying features for the early F-16A/B production blocks (prior to Block 15) visible here include the smaller area horizontal stabilators and blade antenna underneath the air intake. (NARA)

Four 35th TFS F-16A Block 15s during Team Spirit '85. The 35th TFS had upgraded from the Block 10 to the Block 15, the definitive F-16A/B sub-variant, during 1982. Visible Block 15 identifying features compared with earlier blocks include the extended horizontal stabilators (known as the 'big tail', which improved stability, including allowing stable flight at higher angles of attack) and two side-by-side radar warning antennas added under the nose, replacing the blade antenna underneath the air intake. (NARA)

An 80th TFS, 8th TFW, F-4D hauling a varied load during 1980. It carries two 370 US gallon external fuel tanks, a GBU-12 Paveway I 500 lb laser-guided bomb (LGB) under the port wing, a Pave Spike laser designator pod recessed in the port forward Sparrow well, an AN/ALQ-119 ECM pod recessed in the starboard forward Sparrow well, an SUU-21/A practice bomb dispenser under the starboard wing and a centreline SUU-23 20mm gun pod. (NARA)

An 80th TFS F-16A Block 15 taking off from Kunsan AB during Team Spirit '82, with a CATM-9P on the starboard wingtip and a CATM-9L on the port wingtip. (NARA)

Two 80th TFS F-16As taxi out at Kunsan on 19 July 1982 before escorting the last four ex-8th TFW F-4Ds out of the air base at the start of their flight back to the United States. In the foreground is F-16A Block 10 serial 80-0511, while in the background is F-16A Block 15 serial 80-0579, which happens to be the same aircraft seen in the previous image. Although not all are visible here, both aircraft carry a centreline 300 US gallon external fuel tank and a CATM-9L on the starboard wingtip. (NARA)

The two F-16As seen in the previous image escort the last four former 8th TFW F-4Ds out of Kunsan on 19 July 1982. The F-4Ds, which have had all their former unit markings removed, were returning to the United States for reassignment to Air National Guard units. (NARA)

An 80th TFS F-16A Block 10 drops two live Mk 84 2,000-lb bombs during a 14 July 1982 training sortie. (NARA)

Four F-16A Block 15s, three from the 80th TFS and (background) one 35th TFS example, during a tactical large-force employment exercise on 2 December 1983. (NARA)

F-16A Block 15 80-0580, with its serial presentation adapted to act as the 80th TFS squadron commander's jet, seen during Team Spirit '86. When the F-16 was introduced to the 8th TFW, a 'Wolf Cranium' (wolf's head) marking was added to the forward fuselage side. Initially, these were rather crudely painted but were later refined into the definitive form seen here. (NARA)

Four 36th TFS, 51st TFW F-4Es in formation during Team Spirit '84. They each carry an AN/ALQ-119 ECM pod, a CATM-9P and two 370 US gallon external fuel tanks. (NARA)

Three 36th TFS F-4Es carrying AN/ALQ-119 ECM pods and an Air Combat Maneuvering Instrumentation (ACMI) pod during April 1984. An instrumented ACMI range was established in South Korea in 1982. (NARA)

F-4E 68-0421 of the 36th TFS in flight during April 1984. Due to the squadron's primary air-defence tasking, its aircraft often operated without fuel tanks and carried CATM-9s (and ACMI pods after the range was established) in order to hone their air combat skills off Korea's west coast. This aircraft was one of thirty ex-USAF F-4Es transferred to the ROKAF in 1989. (NARA)

F-4Es of the 36th TFS taxi to Osan's runway during exercise Cope Max '85. (NARA)

Throughout the 1980s the wing underwent considerable reorganisation and re-equipment and went on to control several GSUs.

Firstly, the 5th Tactical Air Control Group (TAIRCG) was activated on 8 January 1980 under 51st COMPW; 5th TAIRCG took control of 19th TASS (which at that time adopted a squadron colour, blue). Initially, 5th TAIRCG acted as an intermediate command tier between wing and squadron. However, on 20 June 1982 5th TAIRCG was transferred from 51st COMPW and reassigned directly to 314th AD. As well as being assigned 19th TASS, 5th TAIRCG also controlled several non-flying units, including those operating ground-based radars and FACs.

As noted above, on 1 February 1981 the 25th TFS was transferred without personnel or equipment from the 18th TFW at Kadena (q.v.) and was reassigned to the 51st COMPW as a GSU at Suwon AB, South Korea, activating as an A-10A squadron (but not actually receiving its A-10As until January 1982). The 25th TFS adopted the green squadron tail-stripe colour and initially used the wing's 'OS' tail code; it switched to the 'SU' tail code, reflecting its location at Suwon, on 1 January 1984. In the event of a North Korean invasion of the South, the squadron's twenty-four A-10As would have been thrown straight into the fight to destroy the hordes of oncoming enemy armoured ground forces, in direct conjunction with Korean-based US Army AH-1S Cobra attack helicopters. Suwon was a ROKAF air base, home to the ROKAF 10th TFW operating F-5A, F-5B and RF-5A Freedom Fighters.

A 19th TASS, 5th TAIRCG, 51st COMPW OV-10A Bronco in flight on 1 April 1980. While other USAF forward air control (FAC) aircraft were at this time finished in overall matt FS 36473 'Light Aircraft Gray' (or 'Counter-Insurgency Gray') with full-colour markings, by the 1980s PACAF had adopted the darker overall FS 36118 'Gunship Gray' scheme with toned-down markings on all of its FAC aircraft, as seen here. (NARA)

A 25th TFS, 51st TFW A-10A Thunderbolt II taxis out for a mission during Cope Thunder '83-1 at Clark AB on 1 November 1982. Initially, the 25th TFS used the wing's 'OS' tail code, as seen here. Barely visible in the left background are Republic of Singapore Air Force Hawker Hunters and a PACAF OV-10A. The A-10 variant of the 'European I' scheme consisted of lustreless FS 36081 dark grey, FS 34102 medium green and FS 34092 dark green. (NARA)

A 25th TFS A-10A in flight on 15 March 1984 during Team Spirit '84, carrying an AN/ALQ-119 ECM pod under the starboard wing. The 25th TFS switched to the 'SU' tail code, as seen here, on 1 January 1984, reflecting that it operated as a geographically separated unit at Suwon AB. (NARA)

A 25th TFS A-10A firing its 30-mm GAU-8/A Avenger cannon at a target on the Koon-ni Range during Team Spirit '86. Koon-ni Range, on South Korea's west coast about 25 miles north-west of Osan, was managed by the 51st TFW's 51st Range Squadron. It was the only controlled, fully scoreable, USAF air-to-ground weapons gunnery range in Korea. (NARA)

Finally, the 497th TFS was reassigned from 8th TFW to 51st COMPW on 1 January 1982. As described previously, when assigned to 8th TFW the 497th TFS was a GSU located at Taegu AB; when reassigned to 51st COMPW the 497th TFS remained at Taegu AB but switched from the 'WP' tail code and red fin stripe to the 'OS' tail code and blue fin stripe on its F-4Ds. In April 1982 the 497th TFS transitioned from F-4Ds to F-4Es and on 7 September 1984 it adopted the 'GU' tail code in place of 'OS', reflecting that it was (as it always had been) actually stationed at Taegu, rather than being co-located with either of the wing headquarters it had been assigned to. A small squadron with only around twelve airframes (half that of most USAF tactical squadrons), it operated in the air superiority role.

A 'European I' camouflaged 497th TFS, 51st TFW F-4E flying during Team Spirit '86. The 497th TFS operated from Taegu AB as another 51st TFW geographically separated unit. On 7 September 1984 it switched from the wing's 'OS' tail code to the 'GU' tail code to reflect its detached basing. (NARA)

CATM-9Ps readied for a 497th TFS F-4E at Taegu during Team Spirit '86. The 497th TFS was provided maintenance support by the 6497th Consolidated Aircraft Maintenance Squadron (CAMS); uniquely, the 6497th CAMS's personnel were provided by the ROKAF rather than the USAF. The 6497th's Korean personnel even accompanied the 497th TFS to Nellis AFB, Nevada, for a Red Flag exercise in the late 1980s. (NARA)

Another 497th TFS F-4E during Team Spirit '86, this aircraft in the then-new 'Hill Gray II' camouflage scheme. This two-tone medium-grey (FS 26270) and dark-grey (FS 26118) scheme was very similar, but not identical, to the three-tone light-, medium- and dark-grey factory-applied F-16 'Egyptian I' scheme. Subsequently, F-16s would adopt the simplified two-tone 'Hill Gray II' scheme by dropping the light-grey undersides in favour of medium grey. This aircraft is 69-0297, but it has had its serial modified to read '497' followed by 'TFS' so it can act as the 497th TFS squadron commander's aircraft. However, it has 'ACFT 297' added to the blue squadron tail stripe to confirm its true identity. It carries a CATM-9P. (NARA)

A 19th TASS, 5th TAIRCG OA-37B Dragonfly landing at Osan during Team Spirit '85. The squadron had transitioned from the OV-10A during 1983, although it would revert to the OV-10A later in 1985. Like other PACAF FACs, their OA-37Bs were finished in overall 'Gunship Gray'. As well as permanent 90-gallon wingtip fuel tanks, four 100-gallon fuel tanks are carried underwing and two LAU-68 rocket launcher pods, each with seven tubes for 2.75-inch unguided rockets. For FAC use white phosphorus (WP) rockets would be employed for target marking. (NARA)

On 1 July 1982, 51st COMPW was redesignated 51st TFW.

As noted above, 5th TAIRCG became independent of 51st COMPW and was reassigned directly to 314th AD on 20 June 1982. 5th TAIRCG's 19th TASS converted from OV-10As to OA-37Bs during 1983, only to transition back to OV-10As in 1985 (retaining the 'OS' tail code and blue squadron colour throughout). The OA-37Bs were passed on to the ROKAF after withdrawal from the 19th TASS.

Lieutenant Colonel William Townsley, 19th TASS OA-37B pilot, consults his map during Team Spirit '85. (NARA)

A 19th TASS OV-10A participating in Cope Max '86 in November 1985 after the squadron reverted to the Bronco. The unit subsequently operated OV-10As in either 'Gunship Gray' or 'European I' (referred to as 'Europe I' when applied to the OV-10), the latter seen here. The OV-10 'Europe I' scheme used the same three colours as the A-10 variant of 'European I'. (NARA)

Having signed a fuel receipt, a 19th TASS OV-10A pilot prepares for a Cope Max '86 mission. (NARA)

A 'Europe I'-camouflaged 19th TASS OV-10A during Team Spirit '86. The OV-10 carried four M60C 7.62-mm machine guns, each with 500 rounds, two in each fuselage-side sponson. Each sponson supported two 600-lb (272 kg) hardpoints; only the inner ones are used here, each carrying a LAU-68 rocket launcher pod. The centreline hardpoint carries an external fuel tank. Not in use here, there was a further hardpoint outboard of the engines under each wing. (NARA)

On 8 September 1986 Seventh Air Force was activated at Osan AB, replacing 314th AD, and subsequently leaving Fifth Air Force with only the Japanese-based units. Therefore, the post-September 1986 development of the above Korean-based units, hitherto under 314th AD, will be described under the Seventh Air Force section.

While the above-mentioned wings were assigned to Fifth Air Force via an intermediate Air Division, there were two further wings that were assigned directly to Fifth Air Force: the 432d TFW and 475th Air Base Wing (ABW).

As well as modernising and expanding PACAF in Korea, and as part of a wider expansion of PACAF, permanently based fighter units returned to mainland Japan with the reactivation of the 432d TFW ('MJ' tail code) at Misawa AB, in the northern part of the island of Honshu, on 1 July 1984. PACAF fighters had not been permanently stationed in mainland Japan since 1972. The 432d TFW at Misawa faced the powerful Soviet forces based in the Far East. The 432d TFW was eventually assigned two F-16 squadrons, 13th TFS 'Panthers' (black and white checkerboard tail stripe) and 14th TFS 'Samurais' (black and yellow checkerboard tail stripe) during 1985 and 1987 respectively.

Misawa was a USAF air base, but it also hosted other services. At Misawa, the Japan Air Self-Defense Force (JASDF) operated the Kaikai Kokutai (Airborne Early Warning Air Group), which controlled 601 Hikotai (601st Squadron) with E-2Cs and the 3 Kokudan (3rd Air Wing) with two Mitsubishi F-1/T-2 squadrons. Meanwhile,

A 13th TFS, 432d TFW F-16A Block 15 deployed to Clark AB during Cope Max '86. An inert Mk 84 2,000-lb practice bomb is underwing. This F-16A, 83-1109, was the third aircraft of the final F-16A production block (Block 15S, covering serials 83-1107 to 83-1117) ordered by the USAF. Production then switched to the F-16C Block 25, from aircraft 83-1118. (NARA)

A 13th TFS F-16A Block 15 carrying inert training Mk 82 500-lb bombs and a centreline external fuel tank during Cope Thunder '86-3 on 13 January 1986. (NARA)

A 13th TFS F-16C Block 30 carrying CATM-9Ms and a centreline tank during Cope North '87-3 in Japan on 26 May 1987. All previous F-16s used the Pratt & Whitney F100 engine, however, the F-16C/D Block 30/32 introduced the common engine bay compatible with either the 27,600-lb thrust General Electric F110-GE-100 (Block 30) or the 23,770-lb thrust Pratt & Whitney F100-PW-220 (Block 32). By introducing competition for F-16C/D engine orders, the USAF hoped to drive down costs, encourage further development and increase supply. From Blocks 30/32 onwards, the USAF generally assigned the more powerful F110-powered F-16C/Ds to overseas-based units and the F100-powered F-16C/Ds to US-based units. Here the distinctive curved profile of the F110 engine nozzle is seen; the F100 nozzle was straight-sided. (NARA)

within Misawa AB the USN operated NAF Misawa, which primarily accommodated rotational deployments of P-3C squadrons.

The 13th TFS was activated on 1 June 1985 receiving F-16A/B Block 15s (which had been transferred from TAC's 363d TFW at Shaw AFB, South Carolina). In 1987 13th TFS transitioned to brand-new and much-improved F-16C/D Block 30s.

The 14th TFS was activated on 1 January 1987, and was assigned factory-fresh F-16C/D Block 30s from the outset. Both squadrons primarily operated in the air-defence role, with a secondary ground-attack tasking.

Finally, under Fifth Air Force was 475th Air Base Wing (ABW) at Yokota AB, Japan, where it acted as the host unit. It was directly assigned CT-39A operational support

Two 14th TFS, 432d TFW F-16C
Block 30s with two JASDF F-15Js
during Cope North '88-3 on 17 June
1988. The F-15Js are from the 201
Hikotai, 2 Kokutan from Chitose,
under the Hokubu Koku Homentai.
(NARA)

airlift aircraft (until 1 August 1984 when they were absorbed by MAC's 1403d Military Airlift Squadron (q.v.)) and UH-1Ps, which were replaced by UH-1Ns during 1980 and which it retained beyond the 1980s. The 475th ABW supported Military Airlift Command's resident 316th Tactical Airlift Group and later the 374th Tactical Airlift Wing, which replaced the former at Yokota during 1989.

Seventh Air Force

Seventh Air Force (7 AF), headquartered at Osan AB, South Korea, activated on 8 September 1986. It assumed responsibility for PACAF units on the Korean Peninsula, replacing Fifth Air Force's 314th AD, which, as detailed above, had controlled those units until then.

Following its reassignment from 5 AF/314 AD to 7 AF, the 8th TFW's two squadrons at Kunsan AB transitioned from the F-16A/B Block 15 to the F-16C/D Block 30. The 35th TFS transitioned to the F-16C/D Block 30 during November 1987; the 80th TFS transitioned to the F-16C/D Block 30 during the period February–April 1988. The F-16C/D Block 30s assigned to the 8th TFW featured the enlarged 'big-mouth' inlet introduced part-way through Block 30 production (from Block 30D). Formally known as the modular common inlet duct, this allowed the General Electric F110-GE-100 engine to produce its full thrust at lower air speeds. The 8th TFW retained its

F-16A Block 15s of the 80th TFS,
8th TFW, on the Clark flight line
while deployed for Cope Thunder
'86-1. (NARA)

An 80th TFS F-16A Block 15 during Cope Thunder '86-1. It carries a training CATM-9L/M, an inert Mk 84 practice bomb and a centreline external fuel tank. (NARA)

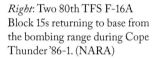

Right: Two 80th TFS F-16A Block 15s returning to base from the bombing range during Cope Thunder '86-1. (NARA)

Below: An 80th TFS F-16A Block 15 during exercise Cobra Gold '87 in July 1987. The wing's 'Wolf Cranium' marking, previously on the forward fuselage side, had by now been moved to the top of the tail. Note the open split speed brakes. (NARA)

air-defence, conventional-attack and nuclear-strike responsibilities after upgrading to the F-16C/D.

The 51st TFW at Osan AB retained the 25th TFS at Suwon AB (A-10As with 'SU' tail code and green tail stripe), 36th TFS at Osan AB (F-4Es with 'OS' tail code and red tail stripe) and 497th TFS (F-4Es with 'GU' tail code and blue tail stripe) at Taegu

Λ 25th TFS, 51st TFW A-10A approaches a highway landing strip during Team Spirit '89. The dispersal of combat aircraft away from airfields to operate from highway strips may have been essential to their survival, and the sustainment of combat operations, in wartime. (NARA)

A 19th TASS, 5th TAIRCG OV-10A pilot and observer prepare for take-off while deployed to Misawa during Orient Shield, part of Cope North 89-1, on 15 December 1988. OV-10As routinely flew with only a pilot and an empty back seat. At this time the squadron operated seventeen OV-10As. (NARA)

The 19th TASS OV-10A seen in the previous image taxis out at Misawa for its mission. Visible in the background are 18th TFW F-15s and RF-4Cs. (NARA)

AB. The 25th TFS retained its A-10As for the remainder of the decade; the 36th TFS transitioned from the F-4E to the F-16C/D Block 30 during 1989 with the first arriving on 6 January, completing conversion in June; the 497th TFS retained its F-4Es until the squadron inactivated on 24 January 1989, subsequently leaving the 51st TFW with two squadrons.

The 5th TAIRCG remained at Osan AB with its OV-10A-equipped 19th TASS, until both group and squadron moved to Suwon AB on 1 August 1989; the 19th TASS then replaced its 'OS' tail code with the 'SU' tail code while retaining the blue stripe and transitioned at that time from OV-10As to OA-10As (operating them alongside the A-10As of the 51st TFW/25th TFS, which were 'SU' coded with a green tail stripe, as noted above).

The final unit assigned to Seventh Air Force during the 1980s was the 460th TRG, which activated on 1 October 1989 at Taegu AB and was assigned the 15th TRS, which, as noted above, had moved with its RF-4Cs to Taegu from Kadena on the same date, after reassignment from the 18th TFW. The 15th TRS adopted the 'GU' tail code in place of their former 'ZZ' code when reassigned. Moving the 15th TRS to Korea from Okinawa achieved several objectives. It maintained Taegu as a main operating base following the inactivation of the F-4E-equipped 497th TFS there on 24 January 1989, as described above. Meanwhile, it permanently located the unit in its intended wartime operating area facing North Korea while reducing PACAF's TDY costs as the unit had previously maintained a permanent forward detachment at Osan AB in Korea (under Det 1, 18th TFW) before the full squadron was permanently moved to Korea.

Thirteenth Air Force

Thirteenth Air Force (13 AF), headquartered at Clark AB, Luzon, Philippines, controlled PACAF units in the Philippines.

Thirteenth Air Force's primary asset was the 3d TFW, which mainly operated F-4s in the air-defence, strike (including precision-strike) and defence-suppression roles. At the start of the decade the 3d TFW ('PN' tail code) at Clark AB was assigned the following: 3d TFS 'Peugeots' (blue); the 90th TFS 'Pair o' Dice' (red); the 1st Test Squadron (TESTS); the non-flying 3d Tactical Electronic Warfare Training Squadron (TEWTS) and the 26th Tactical Fighter Training Aggressor Squadron (TFTAS) 'Aggressors', the latter not adopting the 'PN' tail code or a squadron colour unlike the 3d TFS and 90th TFS. Later in the 1980s the 3d TFS and 90th TFS lost their individual squadron fin-stripe colours and both adopted a red, white and blue 'stars and stripes' fin marking.

The 3d TFS operated late-production F-4Es (FY 71 and later), equipped with the ASX-1 Target Identification Sensor, Electro-Optical (TISEO) pod on the left wing's leading edge. TISEO was intended to identify air-to-air targets beyond visual range but saw greater use identifying navigational waypoints during air-to-ground use. From around 1981 the squadron received F-4Es retrofitted with the AN/ARN-101 DMAS. Known as 'Arnie', this replaced the analogue systems with integrated digital ones, greatly improving navigation and air-to-ground accuracy, while reducing the burden on the crew. The 'Arnie' upgrade also allowed the 3d TFS to employ the GBU-15 modular guided-weapons system (MGWS) 'glide bomb', which entered USAF service during 1983. Depending on the target, the GBU-15 utilised either a 2,000-lb Mk 84 general-purpose warhead or a BLU-109 penetrating warhead; initially the GBU-15 was equipped with a daytime-only electro-optical (EO) sensor; later an alternative day/night/adverse-weather imaging infrared (IIR) seeker became available. GBU-15 could be dropped in a direct-attack 'lock on and launch' mode, like the original Vietnam-era GBU-8, where the bomb was locked on target before launch and could not be controlled after the bomb was released. However, with the launching aircraft equipped with the AN/AXQ-14 data-link pod, the GBU-15 could be launched in an indirect-attack 'lock on after launch' mode; this entailed the bomb being released with the target acquired after launch, the bomb being guided all the way to the target over extended ranges. If 'lobbed', depending on launch speed and altitude, a GBU-15 could glide to targets 8 to 12 miles away, greatly improving the survivability of the launching aircraft. The expensive GBU-15 was considered a 'silver bullet', reserved for well-defended priority targets. During 1984 the 3d TFS also received a number of AN/AVQ-26 Pave Tack pods (nicknamed 'Pave Drag' by aircrews due to the amount of drag the large underside pod created when carried), giving the squadron the ability to employ Paveway laser-guided bombs (LGBs). While so-called 'smart bombs', or precision-guided munitions (PGMs), are almost universally carried by USAF tactical aircraft today, during the 1980s tactical aircraft that could deliver PGMs were the rare exception rather than the norm, with most tactical aircraft relying on 'dumb bombs'. Consequently, the 3d TFS was the only PACAF squadron specialising in delivery of PGMs, and one of only a handful in the entire USAF. During the 1980s, apart from PACAF's 3d TFS, the GBU-15 only equipped the 'Arnie-upgraded' F-4Es of TAC's 4th TFW at Seymour Johnson AFB, North Carolina, and USAFE's 52d TFW at Spangdahlem AB, West Germany. The latter subsequently handed over its GBU-15 tasking to the F-111F-equipped 493d TFS, 48th TFW at RAF Lakenheath, UK. Meanwhile, Pave Tack was similarly rarely assigned to

A 3d TFS F-4E, and in the background a 26th TFTAS F-5E, both of the 3d TFW, in formation on 22 January 1981. The SEA-camouflaged F-4E's tail code (officially known as 'Distinctive Unit Aircraft Identification Markings') and other markings are in white. To reduce visibility USAF tactical aircraft switched from these white markings to black during the early 1980s. The F-5E (74-1574, 'Red 74') displays one of the many varied 'aggressor' camouflage schemes which mimicked those of potential adversaries. This scheme, nicknamed 'grape', consisted of upper sides in FS 35109 international blue, FS 35164 intermediate blue and FS 35414 blue green and FS 35622 duck-egg blue undersides. (NARA)

units; apart from PACAF's 3d TFS, the only USAF strike aircraft to be so equipped were the F-111Fs of USAFE's 48th TFW (the F-111F having the advantage of internal carriage of the pod, mitigating the drag associated with Pave Tack when carried externally on F-4s). Two USAF ARN-101-upgraded RF-4C reconnaissance squadrons (TAC's 12th TRS, 67th TRW at Bergstrom AFB, Texas, and USAFE's 1st TRS, 10th TRW at RAF Alconbury, UK) were also assigned Pave Tack. These RF-4Cs primarily used Pave Tack as a reconnaissance sensor, but also for target laser designation for strike aircraft in the Strike Control and Reconnaissance (SCAR) role. PACAF's 15th TRS was not Pave Tack-equipped, however. Therefore, the 3d TFS's PGM guidance and delivery capabilities were unique within PACAF and of critical importance to the command.

The 90th TFS operated a mixed fleet of F-4Es and F-4Gs in the 'Wild Weasel' suppression of enemy air defences (SEAD) role, although its F-4Es also undertook the air-to-air role. A dozen F-4Gs had been assigned to the squadron from 1979 onwards, joining a similar number of F-4Es. Together they operated in teams as hunter-killer pairs, the F-4G detecting hostile radar sites which both the F-4G and F-4E could attack with specialised anti-radiation missiles (ARMs) or conventional munitions such as cluster-bomb units (CBUs).

A 3d TFS F-4E participating in Cope North '80. The white tail code and markings have been replaced by black ones. It retains full-colour national insignia; later these would also be toned down to further reduce visibility. (NARA)

A 3d TFS F-4E pilot discusses aircraft maintenance before a Cope North '80 mission while deployed to Misawa. (NARA)

A 3d TFS F-4E deployed to Osan during Team Spirit '84. In the foreground is a Triple Ejector Rack (TER) carrying two live Mk 82 low-drag, general-purpose (LDGP) bombs (a third could be loaded on the TER's underside). This TER presumably awaits another F-4E, as TERS carrying blue Mk 82 practice bombs are just visible under the wing of this F-4E. The ASX-1 TISEO pod equipped all 3d TFS F-4Es, as seen here on the wing leading edge with a yellow protective cover fitted. (NARA)

A 3d TFS F-4E drops a GBU-15 'glide bomb' during Team Spirit '85, demonstrating the squadron's role as PACAF's PGM delivery specialists. This is a GBU-15(V)1/B with a Mk 84 warhead, 'long-chord' wings and a daytime-only electro-optical (EO) seeker head. Just visible on the F-4E's centreline is the AN/AXQ-14 data-link pod, via which the GBU-15 was controlled after release. The expensive GBU-15 was intended to be used sparingly, targeting only well-defended, high-value targets. (NARA)

On 26 August 1981 a SAC SR-71 flying a reconnaissance sortie along the South Korean side of the Korean demilitarised zone (DMZ) was fired upon by a North Korean SA-2 surface-to-air missile (the SAM missed the SR-71 by 2 miles); the sortie had been targeting the site the SAM had been fired from, which had been suspected to be an SA-2 site under construction, but which had clearly become operational! As a consequence, 90th TFS F-4Gs were deployed to South Korea in a plan approved by President Reagan. Four additional SR-71 missions would be flown along the DMZ during October which required the SR-71 to pass above the offending SAM site within a strict 30-second time-over-target (TOT) window. Meanwhile, the F-4Gs would orbit at low level near the DMZ armed with live ARMs and CBUs, ready to pop up and strike the North Korean SAM site within

Ground crewmen refuel a 'Hill Gray II'-camouflaged 3d TFS F-4E at Clark on 1 December 1989. Late in the decade, the 3d TFW replaced the individual squadron tail-stripe colours with the 'stars and stripes' markings seen here. (NARA)

A 90th TFS F-4G 'Advanced Wild Weasel V' in flight on 22 January 1981. It carries an AN/ALQ-119 ECM pod recessed in the port forward Sparrow well, an SUU-21/A practice bomb dispenser under the port wing and a centreline fuel tank. (NARA)

An immaculate 90th TFS F-4G deployed to Korea for Team Spirit '82. It features wraparound SEA camouflage, with toned-down national markings. Where its outer underwing hardpoints have been removed the original light-grey underside colour is visible. Underwing TERs carry four live Mk 82 LDGP bombs. The F-4G introduced the F-15's 'high g' 600 US gallon external fuel tank in lieu of the usual centreline F-4 600 US gallon tank, a feature later extended to other USAF Phantoms. This allowed heavily laden F-4Gs to violently pop up to acquire their targets and dip back down to low level again. (NARA)

A 90th TFS F-4E (top) and F-4G (bottom) viewed from a KC-135 boom operator's position on 18 October 1984. The F-4E's refuelling receptacle is open. The F-4E carries two 370 US gallon external fuel tanks and an SUU-21/A practice bomb pod. The F-4G carries an ATM-45 (captive training version of the AGM-45 Shrike anti-radiation missile) and an SUU-21/A. It also presumably carries a centreline 600 US gallon external fuel tank. Both carry AN/ALQ-119 ECM pods. (NARA)

A 90th TFS F-4E, operating from Takhli Royal Thai Air Force (RTAF) Base, in formation with an RTAF F-5F on 15 October 1984 during exercise Commando West VIII. Both aircraft carry practice CATM-9J/Ps. (NARA)

Another 90th TFS F-4E at Takhli during Commando West VIII. Note the lack of TISEO pod on the leading edge of the starboard wing. While the 3d TFS operated late-production F-4Es with TISEO, the 90th TFS operated earlier production models which lacked them. (NARA)

60 seconds of a hostile SAM launch against the SR-71. The tight 30-second SR-71 TOT ensured that the F-4Gs would be headed in the direction of the SAM site north of the DMZ at the critical moment. The four missions passed off without any further hostilities from the North Koreans.

Between 1 and 9 December 1989 members of the Armed Forces of the Philippines, including elements of the Philippine Air Force, staged an attempted coup against Philippine President Aquino. These rebel forces belonged to the Reform the Armed Forces Movement (RAM) as well as personnel loyal to former President Marcos. A number of Philippine military bases fell under the control of, or were attacked by, rebel forces. Rebel T-28 Trojans attacked various targets, including Malacañang Palace, the principal workplace and official residence of the president. With loyal forces struggling to contain the rebels, Aquino requested US military assistance, which President Bush authorised. US military intervention, conducted under Operation Classic Resolve, aimed to deter the rebels while avoiding direct confrontation, and largely involved air power, although 100 US Marines did deploy from the USN base at Subic Bay to protect the US Embassy in Manila. US air power was provided by the 3d TFW's F-4s as well as the USN aircraft carriers USS *Midway* and USS *Enterprise*, which conducted flight operations in the area, including providing continuous radar coverage of the Manila Bay area with their E-2Cs, supporting the USAF and USN air operations. The primary aim of Operation Classic Resolve was to deter rebel aircraft from taking off and attacking Manila. On the first day of the coup attempt, 1 December, the 3d TFW went on immediate alert duty and scrambled F-4s, which flew patrols over rebel Philippine Air Force bases, demonstrating what then Chairman of the Joint Chiefs of Staff General Colin Powell described as 'extreme hostile intent'. As well as aggressively 'buzzing' the rebel air bases, they were instructed to fire their guns ahead of any aircraft that attempted to taxi for take-off and shoot down any rebel aircraft that did take off. The 3d TFS initially loaded up with dumb bombs before switching to GBU-10 Paveway II laser-guided bombs and high-explosive incendiary (HEI) ammunition in their 20mm M61A1 guns. In the initial rush, the 90th TFS didn't have time to load missiles and scrambled F-4Es just with Training Practice (TP) ammunition in the M61A1 gun; subsequently, it launched F-4Es armed with live AIM-7 and AIM-9 air-to-air missiles and HEI ammunition in the gun. No shots were fired by 3d TFW F-4s during these operations, and loyal forces defeated the coup attempt by 9 December 1989.

The 1st TESTS and 3d TEWTS were reassigned from the 3d TFW to the 6200th Tactical Fighter Training Group (TFTG) on 1 January 1980, and will therefore be discussed below.

The 26th TFTAS operated T-38As and F-5Es in the 'aggressor' dissimilar air-combat-training (DACT) role; in 1980 it operated four T-38As and was in the process of building its F-5E fleet up to an eventual total of ten airframes. It ceased T-38A operations on 25 November 1980, subsequently operating just F-5Es, with the fleet being maintained at ten airframes, with nine intended to be operational at any one time. On 22 April 1983 it was redesignated the 26th Aggressor Squadron (AS). The 26th AS was due to transition from F-5Es to F-16C Block 30s and move to Kadena at the end of the decade; the squadron ceased F-5E operations during 1988 and was reassigned to the 18th TFW and moved to Kadena without aircraft on 1 October 1988. The squadron's personnel had largely completed F-16 training by 1989 and the unit was awaiting its new equipment.

T-38A 65-10409 'Red 09' of the 26th TFTAS. The scheme is 'Old Blue', featuring the same colours as the 'grape' scheme mentioned previously, but in a different pattern. (NARA)

Major John Corky briefs 26th AS F-5E pilots at Clark during Cope Thunder '84-7 on 10 September 1984. (NARA)

Nine new-production F-16C Block 30s (the final Block 30s built) eventually arrived at Kadena in a mixture of 'Fulcrum' and 'Flogger' schemes in the period August–September 1989. However, by the time they arrived the decision had been made to curtail the USAF aggressor programme and the squadron never stood up again as an operational F-16C aggressor squadron. Consequently, the F-16Cs were reassigned to the 8th TFW at Kunsan, where they were eventually repainted in the standard F-16 grey camouflage scheme, and the 26th AS was inactivated on 21 February 1990.

F-5E 74-1575 'Red 75' of the 26th AS taxiing out for a Cope Thunder '84-7 mission on 10 September 1984. It features the 'Old Blue' scheme and carries a CATM-9J/P. (NARA)

The 26th AS commander's overall silver F-5E, 74-1389 'Red 26', prepares for a mission during Cope Thunder '84-7. Other 26th AS aircraft used the last two numbers of their serial for their Soviet-style 'bort number'. However, as the 26th AS's commander's aircraft 74-1389 became 'Red 26' (rather than 'Red 89') to reflect the squadron, the bort number was modified to read '26TH AGGRESSOR COMMANDER'. The F-5E featured two-position nose gear, which when extended, as here, increased the wing angle of attack on the ground by approximately 3.1 degrees, improving take-off performance. (NARA)

Five 26th AS F-5E pilots perform their final checks before a mission during Cope Thunder '84-7. (NARA)

F-5E 75-0613 'Red 13' of the 26th AS approaching the Clark runway at the conclusion of a Cope Thunder '84-7 mission, carrying a CATM-9J/P. It is in the 'Frog' scheme, consisting of FS 30111 maroon olympic russet, FS 33717 sand and FS 34052 Marine Corps green topsides with FS 36622 camouflage-grey undersides. (NARA)

Overall-silver 26th AS F-5E 74-1388 'Red 88' during a Cope Thunder mission in 1987. (NARA)

An MC-130E Combat Talon I and personnel of the 1st SOS during a welcoming ceremony at Clark on 15 January 1981, the squadron having just transferred from the 18th TFG at Kadena to Clark's 3d TFW. The MC-130E displays the unique Combat Talon I black-and-green camouflage scheme, and the standard 'Pinocchio' nose of PACAF's 'Yank' sub-variant, as opposed to the Fulton STARS gear and chin radome of the TAC/USAFE Combat Talon I 'Clamp' sub-variant. (NARA)

A 3d TFW T-33A Shooting Star leads two RAAF Mirage IIIOs over Luzon on 12 November 1981 during a Cope Thunder exercise. The left RAAF Mirage is from No. 3 Squadron, based at Butterworth in Malaysia, while the right Mirage is from No. 75 Squadron, based at Williamtown, Australia. (NARA)

An overall-FS 16473 'Aircraft Gray' 3d TFW T-33A prepares for a Cope Thunder '83-7 mission from Clark on 15 September 1983. (NARA)

As noted above, the 1st Special Operations Squadron, under the 18th TFG, moved with its MC-130Es from Kadena to Clark on 1 January 1981. It was reassigned to the 3d TFW on 15 January 1981. On 1 March 1983 Military Airlift Command activated Twenty-Third Air Force (23 AF), which took over USAF special operations (and other) units from various MAJCOMs, consolidating them under a single command. Consequently, while it remained stationed at Clark AB, the 1st SOS was reassigned from PACAF's 3d TFW to MAC's 23 AF on 1 March 1983, initially being assigned to 23 AF's 2d Air Division (Hurlburt Field, Florida).

A small number of T-33As were directly assigned to the 3d TFW at Clark until 1987, primarily providing adversary and target support for Cope Thunder exercises, which are described below. CT-39A operational support airlift aircraft were also directly assigned to 3d TFW until 1 October 1984, when they were absorbed by MAC's Det 1, 1403d Military Airlift Squadron (q.v.). From 1988 UH-1Ns were directly assigned to 3d TFW to support Cope Thunder.

The 6200th Tactical Fighter Training Group (TFTG) was also directly assigned to 13 AF and had been activated at Clark AB on 1 September 1977. The 6200th TFTG was responsible for administering two programmes, Cope Thunder and Combat Sage.

Cope Thunder had been established by PACAF at Clark AB in 1976 as PACAF's premier air-combat training exercise; the realistic, ten-day exercise was held up to four times per year. Units from throughout the Pacific area participated in Cope Thunder, not just those of PACAF, but also aircraft from other USAF MAJCOMs as well as aircraft from the US Navy, US Marine Corps and some foreign allied air forces. Cope Thunder was conducted over a large area, with the exercise's airspace covering almost half the length of Luzon, from Crow Valley 10 miles north of Clark AB and extending 100 miles northwards from there. Crow Valley was the location of the main United States Armed Forces bombing range in the western Pacific, Crow Valley Gunnery Range, which contained bombing targets and scoring systems. In a typical Cope Thunder exercise, friendly 'blue' forces would operate from Clark AB, proceed up through central Luzon, then turn south to pass through the exercise airspace to attack the targets in Crow Valley. 'Enemy' ('red') forces, which often included USN aircraft as well as the 26th TFTAS/AS T-38As and F-5Es and 3d TFW T-33As, stood

US Marines launch a GTR-18A Smokey Sam, which visually simulated a surface-to-air missile launch, as an aircraft approaches the Crow Valley Gunnery Range during Cope Thunder '84-7. In the foreground is a portable radar unit and an M151 ¼-ton 4×4 utility truck. The Crow Valley Gunnery Range was operated by the 3d TEWTS, 6200th TFTG. (NARA)

in the way of the blue forces in the exercise, as did an array of radar transmitters that replicated Soviet surface-to-air (SAM) missile radars and radar-controlled anti-aircraft artillery (AAA).

The Combat Sage Weapons System Evaluation Program (WSEP) evaluated the capabilities of PACAF fighter squadrons to fire air-to-air missiles (AAMs). PACAF fighter squadrons regularly deployed to Clark to launch AAMs at target drones which were launched from the Drone Launch Facility at Wallace Air Station, the latter being a small installation north of Clark AB. The AAMs fired were otherwise live, although their warheads were replaced by telemetry packages which transmitted data to Combat Sage telemetry-gathering stations which recorded missile performance, pilot performance and miss distance. Consequently, missile-, aircraft- and pilot-performance data was collated and analysed, allowing for improvements of aircraft and missile systems as well as pilot training programmes. Combat Sage supported F-4-equipped units, as well as F-15 units from 1980 and F-16 units from 1982.

The 1st Test Squadron (TESTS) was reassigned from the 3d TFW to the 6200th TFTG on 1 January 1980. The 1st TESTS supported the Combat Sage WSEP; it borrowed 3d TFW F-4Es as required and also operated BQM-34A Firebee remotely piloted vehicle (RPV) target drones from Wallace Air Station's Drone Launch Facility; in 1989 the BQM-34As were replaced by MQM-107 Streaker target drones. The drones were usually recoverable after parachuting into the sea at the end of their mission. Therefore, MAC HH-3Es from Clark AB (see below) and a drone recovery boat (homeported at nearby San Fernando) were always on hand to recover the drones.

The 3d Tactical Electronic Warfare Training Squadron (TEWTS) was a non-flying unit and was also reassigned from the 3d TFW to the 6200th TFTG on 1 January 1980. It operated Camp O'Donnell, Philippines, which housed the PACAF Electronic Warfare Range, the Crow Valley Gunnery Range and other associated facilities that supported the Cope Thunder exercises.

Direct Reporting Units

Besides those units assigned to 5 AF, 7 AF and 13 AF, several units reported directly to PACAF headquarters at Hickam AFB, Hawaii.

The 15th Air Base Wing at Hickam AFB provided base-level support for headquarters PACAF. It was also the host organisation not only for Hickam AFB but also managed Wheeler AFB, Oahu, Hawaii, and Wake Island, plus several smaller subsidiary bases including Bellows Air Force Station (AFS), Oahu, Hawaii, which was a former airfield primarily operated as an Armed Forces Recreation Center. The 15th ABW's 15th Air Base Squadron (ABS) acted as host at Wheeler AFB, while Detachment 4, 15th Air Base Wing was responsible for Wake Island (not only its airfield but also the island's civil administration). The 15th ABW controlled two flying squadrons, the 9th Airborne Command and Control Squadron (ACCS) and the 22d TASS.

The 9th ACCS at Hickam AFB operated EC-135Js in the BLUE EAGLE Airborne Command Post (ABNCP) role, supporting Commander in Chief, Pacific Fleet (CINCPAC) and also operating as a VIP transport for the PACAF commander. The EC-135J's 'front-end crew' consisted of pilot, co-pilot, navigator and a boom operator (the EC-135Js retained a refuelling boom and could act as tankers). The 'back-end crew' consisted of two radio operators, a cryptographic teletype operator, a radio maintenance technician and the CINCPAC battle staff, usually led by a USN captain. At the start of the decade three EC-135Js were assigned (serial numbers 63-8055, 63-8056 and 63-8057). An EC-135C (62-3584) had also been assigned to the unit since 1977 for use as a trainer, however this had been transferred to E-Systems for conversion into the BLUE EAGLE configuration in late 1979 and was returned to the 9th ACCS during February 1980 as their fourth EC-135J. The EC-135Js sat remote alert at air bases throughout the PACAF area. In June 1980 a computer malfunction issued an erroneous message that the United States was under attack which resulted in a BLUE EAGLE EC-135J launching as per protocols. Once the message was confirmed as being erroneous, and that the situation was actually all clear, the EC-135J returned to base. However, this demonstrated the quick reaction of the BLUE EAGLE mission.

The 22d TASS (blue fin-cap marking) operated O-2As from Wheeler AFB; the squadron was reassigned to the 326th Air Division on 4 April 1980 (q.v.).

A number of T-33As were directly assigned to the 15th ABW at Hickam AFB for Hawaii adversary/target support work.

Two 9th ACCS, 15th ABW EC-135J airborne command posts seen during 1987, showing off their ability to also act as tankers as 62-3584 prepares to refuel 63-8056. (NARA)

The 326th Air Division at Wheeler AFB was also directly assigned to PACAF. It coordinated Hawaii's air defences via the (non-flying) 6010th and 6491st Aerospace Defense Flights.

The 326th AD expanded its mission when the 22d TASS was reassigned to it on 4 April 1980, as mentioned above. The 22d TASS transitioned from O-2As to OV-10As during 1983, and at that time adopted the WH tail code while retaining the blue squadron colour. On 22 September 1988 22d TASS inactivated.

During 1983 the 326th AD extended its air-defence responsibilities to also cover the Mariana Islands, including Guam; during 1984 the 326th AD's air-defence system was upgraded from a manual to an automated system when its Regional Operations Control Center (ROCC) was established.

The 326th AD inactivated on 15 February 1989. At that time the 6010th Aerospace Defense Flight was expanded to become the 6010th Aerospace Defense Group and took over the 326th AD's former air-defence responsibilities; the 326th AD's other responsibilities were passed to the 15th ABW.

A 22d TASS, 326th AD, OV-10A at Wheeler AFB, Hawaii, on 22 August 1984 during exercise Opportune Journey '84. It features PACAF's usual overall 'Gunship Gray' FAC scheme with toned-down markings. A US Army UH-1H helicopter is in flight in the background. (NARA)

A crew chief stands by in front of 22d TASS OV-10As deployed to Osan for Team Spirit '85. In the background two locally based 36th TFS F-4Es launch on a mission, the trail Phantom still in afterburner. (NARA)

Alaskan Air Command

At the start of the 1980s Alaskan Air Command (AAC), headquartered at Elmendorf AFB, Alaska, had its flying units split between the 21st TFW at Elmendorf AFB and the 5010th Combat Support Group (CSG) at Eielson AFB, Alaska.

In 1980 the 21st TFW at Elmendorf used the 'FC' tail code and was directly assigned T-33As to provide local adversary and air-defence training target support work, as well as a C-12A light transport which had been reassigned to 21st TFW from the 343d TFG (see below) when the latter inactivated on 1 January 1980. The 21st TFW relinquished its T-33As and C-12A to the newly established 5021st Tactical Operations Squadron during 1981 (see below). Two F-4E squadrons were assigned – 18th TFS 'Blue Foxes' and 43d TFS Hornets'. During the late 1970s the 18th TFS used white tail stripes and the 43d TFS used gold; sometime around 1980 both squadrons adopted blue tail stripes with four gold stars, along with a blue rudder featuring a white polar bear. Until 1 January 1980 there was an intermediate group (the 343d TFG) between the two squadrons and the 21st TFW wing headquarters; when the 343d TFG inactivated on 1 January 1980 the 18th TFS and 43d TFS were reassigned directly to the 21st TFW. The F-4Es operated in both the air-defence and air-to-ground roles, the latter primarily being to provide close air support (CAS) for US Army units in Alaska. As well as maintaining aircraft on air-defence alert at Elmendorf, other 21st TFW aircraft were forward-deployed to air-defence-alert, forward-operating locations (FOLs) at Eielson AFB, King Salmon AFS and Galena AFS. The 21st TFW's air-defence responsibilities covered a vast area, from the North Pole to the Aleutian Islands.

On 1 October 1981 the 5021st Tactical Operations Squadron (TOS) was activated at Elmendorf and assigned to the 21st TFW; it absorbed the T-33As and C-12A

An 18th TFS, 343d TFG, 21st TFW F-4E over Mount McKinley on 15 September 1978. On 1 January 1980 the intermediate 343d TFG inactivated; the squadrons subsequently reported directly to the wing. (NARA)

A 21st TFW F-4E taxiing in at Elmendorf streaming its drag chute during exercise Brim Frost '81 in January 1981. It carries two SUU-21/A practice bomb dispensers and three external fuel tanks, and displays the revised markings introduced around 1980: a blue tail stripe with four gold stars and a blue rudder featuring a white polar bear. This was a common marking for all wing aircraft, replacing the previous individual squadron tail-stripe colours. (NARA)

A T-33A of the 5021st TOS, 21st TFW in flight during June 1984, finished in overall FS 16473 Aircraft Gray and lacking Arctic Markings. (NARA)

previously directly assigned to the 21st TFW headquarters and T-33As previously directly assigned to the 5010th CSG headquarters. Their T-33As continued to provide air-defence training target support, however they also had an emergency wartime combat role and aircrew therefore also practised dropping Mk 82 500 lb bombs from the T-33As. The 5021st TOS inactivated on 1 July 1988.

On 1 January 1982 the 18th TFS was transferred without personnel or equipment from the 21st TFW to the recently activated 343d Composite Wing (COMPW) at Eielson AFB, where it was stood up as an A-10A unit (see below).

The 43d TFS transitioned from the F-4E to the F-15A/B from March 1982 (the Eagles coming from Tactical Air Command's 1st TFW at Langley AFB, which was transitioning from the F-15A/B to the F-15C/D). The squadron's final F-4E departed Elmendorf on 16 November 1982. Henceforth the squadron operated purely in the air-to-air role; the CAS role was now covered by the new A-10As of the 18th TFS, 343d COMPW. Upon equipping with F-15A/Bs, the 43d TFS adopted the 'AK' tail code in place of the former 'FC' tail code used by the F-4Es. As the only F-15 squadron in the 21st TFW, the 43d TFS did not initially use a squadron tail stripe colour on its F-15A/Bs. The first 43d TFS intercept of a Soviet aircraft following transition to the F-15A occurred on 24 November 1982 when two F-15As launched from the King Salmon FOL and intercepted a Tu-95KM 'Bear-C'. This was the first time that any F-15s had intercepted a 'Bear'.

Thirteen 5021st TOS T-33As on the Elmendorf flight line on 18 October 1984. They feature high-visibility Arctic Markings, consisting of FS 12197 International Orange on the nose, tail and wingtips. The nearest T-33A carries an underwing AN/ALQ-71 ECM pod, used for their air-defence training target support work; a chaff dispenser was usually carried under the other wing for such missions. (NARA)

Two 43d TFS F-15As take off beyond the 5021st TOS T-33A flight line at Elmendorf. A black AN/ALE-2 chaff dispenser pod is under the T-33's wing. An International Orange personal luggage pod is under the rear fuselage. Barely visible under the left wing is an AN/ALQ-71 ECM pod. (NARA)

During 1987 the 21st TFW's capabilities were considerably enhanced by the introduction of the F-15C/D and the addition of a second squadron. On 8 May 1987 the 54th TFS 'Leopards' was activated (with the 'AK' tail code and yellow squadron tail-stripe colour), equipped with F-15C/Ds received from TAC's 1st TFW, as the latter was upgrading to the improved F-15C/D MSIP sub-variant. During the same time period the 43d TFS also upgraded to F-15C/Ds from the same source, adopting the blue squadron colour at that time. The 43d TFS passed their old F-15A/Bs to the Hawaii Air National Guard's 199th TFS, 154th COMPG at Hickam AFB, the latter using them to replace their F-4Cs. As well as adopting squadron colours following re-equipment with F-15C/Ds, the 21st TFW also added wing markings to the inside faces of both tails, consisting of a wide black band containing yellow stars depicting the Big Dipper and the North Star.

Due to the very large distances covered by the wing, their F-15C/Ds were able to be equipped with range-extending conformal fuel tanks (CFTs) on the fuselage sides, an option not available to F-15A/Bs. Very few USAF F-15C/D units received a supply of CFTs, although the 21st TFW did, as did TAC's 57th Fighter Interceptor Squadron based at Keflavik on Iceland, which similarly covered a very large area with limited divert options.

F-15A 74-0105 of the 43d TFS, 21st TFW seen in June 1984. The Eagle's large wing area instigated one of the type's nicknames, the 'Flying Tennis Court'. (NARA)

Right: A side view of the F-15A seen in the previous image. As the only flying squadron in the 21st TFW at this time, the 43d TFS lacked a squadron tail-stripe colour. Although not all are visible here, this aircraft carries a full load of live AIM-9Ls and AIM-7Fs plus three external fuel tanks. (NARA)

Below: F-15As 74-0105 and 74-0099 of the 43d TFS displaying their live armament. (NARA)

A 43d TFS F-15A tests the Mobile Aircraft Arresting System (MAAS), temporarily installed at the small and remote Deadhorse Airport on Alaska's north coast, during Exercise Cobbler Freeze '87 on 9 March 1987. Arresting systems allow combat aircraft to use their tailhook to land on short, damaged or temporary runways, or during emergencies such as brake or steering failure. MAAS is a mobile trailer-mounted variant of the fixed BAK-12 arresting system used at USAF air bases. Cobbler Freeze '87 was an Alaskan Air Command cold-weather force projection exercise. C-130Es of the 17th TAS had delivered the MAAS and everything from maintenance tents to a tactical air navigation (TACAN) system van to support the deployed F-15s. By this time the 21st TFW had adopted a black panel featuring the Big Dipper and North Star on the inner faces of their F-15s' twin tails. (NARA)

A few months earlier this scene would have been unthinkable, unless war had broken out: 43d TFS F-15s intercepting Soviet MiG-29s approaching Alaska on 1 August 1989. In a rapidly changing world, the MiG-29s (a single-seat MiG-29 'Fulcrum-A' and a two-seat MiG-29UB 'Fulcrum-B') were heading to their first North American appearance at the Abbotsford International Airshow in British Columbia, Canada. This impressive image shows the MiG-29s approaching from the distance while two F-15s are manoeuvring to the intercept. (NARA)

The Soviet MiG-29s being escorted after interception, with the MiG-29UB 'Fulcrum-B' leading the MiG-29 'Fulcrum-A'. The two background F-15Cs are equipped with CFTs and carry full Sparrow and Sidewinder armament. The foreground F-15D lacks CFTs and missiles but carries three external fuel tanks. The Eagles subsequently handed the escort over to Canadian Armed Forces CF-188s (CF-18s). The 43d TFS added the blue squadron tail stripe seen here when it upgraded to F-15C/Ds, coinciding with the addition of a second Eagle squadron (54th TFS) to the 21st TFW in 1987. (NARA)

The 21st TFW's F-15s regularly took part in exercises and deployments, not only the biennial 'Brim Frost' exercises within Alaska, but also exercise 'Team Spirit' in the Republic of Korea and training exercises with the Canadian Forces Air Command.

A notable episode occurred on 1 August 1989 that demonstrated how quickly the world was changing at that time. A pair of Soviet MiG-29s (a single-seat MiG-29 'Fulcrum-A' and a two-seat MiG-29UB 'Fulcrum-B') was heading to their first North American appearance at the Abbotsford International Airshow in Canada. They were initially intercepted by four 21st TFW F-15C/Ds as they approached Alaska, who escorted them and subsequently handed them off to CF-188A/Bs of the Canadian Armed Forces.

Two Air Base Squadrons (ABS) were assigned to the 21st TFW to act as the host units administering the activities and maintenance of the FOLs: the 5071st ABS was the host unit for King Salmon AFS, while the 5072d ABS was the host unit for Galena AFS.

Following the *Exxon Valdez* oil spill on 24 March 1989, AAC and MAC personnel from Elmendorf were involved in the clean-up operation, operating both on the ground and flying in urgently needed supplies to the disaster area, which was in Prince William Sound, 107 miles (172 km) south-east of Elmendorf.

In 1980 the 5010th CSG at Eielson AFB controlled the 25th TASS operating O-2As with Arctic markings of orange panels on the nose, tails and wings. Like the 21st TFW, the 5010th CSG also had directly assigned T-33As, and likewise also relinquished its T-33As to the newly established 5021st TOS during 1981 (see above).

The 343d TFG had inactivated on 1 January 1980 at Elmendorf AFB (where it had acted as an intermediate tier between the wing and the flying squadrons) and was

The first two A-10As (80-0221 and 80-0222) arrived at Eielson AFB from the Fairchild-Republic factory on 18 December 1981, ahead of the activation of the 18th TFS on 1 January 1982. A-10A 80-0221 was soon repainted in an experimental Arctic camouflage scheme for upcoming exercise Cool Snow Hog '82-1 to be held from 8–16 March 1982, at a Forward Operating Location (FOL) at Kotzebue Air Force Station, northwest Alaska. This was the first test of forward basing A-10s in Alaska, and involved two 18th TFS A-10s (the other in standard 'European I' camouflage) flying sixteen CAS sorties in support of the Alaska Army National Guard's 3d Scout Battalion. A-10A 80-0221 is seen in its Arctic scheme (consisting of temporary white stripes painted over the 'European I' scheme) at Kotzebue AFS on 8 March 1982. (NARA)

A four-ship 18th TFS A-10A formation during a 31 May 1982 training mission. At this time the squadron lacked a coloured tail stripe. (NARA)

reactivated on 1 October 1981 and redesignated as the 343d Composite Wing (COMPW) at Eielson AFB, replacing the 5010th CSG and absorbing the latter's personnel and equipment. It was subsequently redesignated the 343d TFW on 8 June 1984.

The 25th TASS was assigned to 343d COMPW when the latter replaced the 5010th CSG; the squadron retained their O-2As with orange panels until July 1986 when the unit transitioned to the OV-10A, at which time they adopted the 'AK' tail code and red squadron colour. The 25th TASS inactivated on 15 September 1989. Throughout its existence the 25th TASS maintained a relatively small complement of between eight and twelve aircraft on strength.

Crewmen wash 18th TFS A-10A 80-0222 on 29 September 1983 while visiting Davis Monthan AFB, Arizona, prior to a 'hop' to Nellis AFB, Nevada, to participate in Gunsmoke '83. The Gunsmoke competition, officially titled the USAF Worldwide Gunnery Meet and conducted every other year, involved challenging two-ship and four-ship bombing and strafing missions. Participating units sent a five-aircraft team (four primary, one spare). Aircraft attending Gunsmoke were expected to be spotless, no doubt accounting for the wash before it deployed to Nellis. Note the red masking used on the forward fuselage and around the canopy while being washed. The blue tail stripe featuring a black fox adopted by the 18th TFS on its A-10As is visible here. (NARA)

An 18th TFS A-10A arrives at Osan, South Korea, on 15 March 1984 to participate in Team Spirit '84. It carries two 600 US gallon ferry tanks, essential for deployment from Alaska to Korea; the F-111 used the same type of tank. (NARA)

A joint US and Korean colour guard marches past 18th TFS pilots and A-10As during Team Spirit '84 at Kimhae AB, a ROKAF air base near Pusan in southern South Korea. (NARA)

As noted above, the 18th TFS transferred without personnel or equipment from the 21st TFW at Elmendorf to the 343d COMPW at Eielson AFB, where it was stood up as an A-10A unit on 1 January 1982. It adopted the 'AK' tail code, later adding a blue tail stripe featuring a black fox on its A-10As. After the 25th TASS inactivated in 1989, a dedicated forward air-control flight was formed within the 18th TFS to take over the responsibilities of the former OV-10A unit.

Assigned directly to the Alaskan Air Command was the 531st Aircraft Control and Warning Group (ACWG) at Elmendorf AFB. The 531st ACWG controlled several Aircraft Control and Warning Squadrons (ACWS) operating a variety of manned surveillance radar and Ground Control Intercept (GCI) radar sites. The 531st ACWG was redesignated the 11th Tactical Control Group on 1 July 1981. The group's Aircraft Control and Warning Squadrons were: the 705th ACWS at King Salmon AFS; 708th ACWS at Indian Mountain AFS; 710th ACWS at Tin City AFS; 711th ACWS at Cape Lisburne AFS; 714th ACWS at Cold Bay AFS; 717th ACWS at Tatalina AFS; 719th ACWS at Sparrevohn AFS; 743d ACWS at Campion AFS; 744th ACWS at Murphy Dome AFS; 748th ACWS at Kotzebue AFS; 794th ACWS at Cape Newenham AFS; and 795th ACWS at Cape Romanzof AFS.

The 531st Aircraft Control and Warning Group had been assigned to the 21st TFW until it was reassigned to direct Alaskan Air Command control on 30 September 1979.

Many of the radar systems operated had been in place since the 1950s. The growing threat presented by the Soviets by the 1980s, including the introduction of Soviet cruise missiles, prompted the re-equipment of these sites with the new AN/FPS-117 radar, as well as a wider improvement to air-defence systems and capabilities. The AN/FPS-117 radar was introduced to the radar sites from 1982 under the 'Seek Igloo' programme (the site at King Salmon having received the prototype AN/FPS-117 during September 1982), replacing the various elderly radar systems. The AN/FPS-117 was intended to be operated remotely and required much less maintenance than the former systems. The system transmitted aircraft tracking data via satellite to the Elmendorf Region Operations Control Center (ROCC), which reached initial operational capability (IOC) on 15 June 1983 and full operational status on 15 September 1983; it was jointly operated by US and Canadian personnel due to the NORAD arrangements

An 18th TFS A-10A participating in the USAF-US Army combined-arms live-fire exercise CALFEX IV at the Yukon Command Training Site, Alaska, on 20 September 1988. (NARA)

(see below). The ROCC was redesignated the Sector Operations Control Center (SOCC) on 1 October 1986.

Due to the much-reduced manning requirements, the individual radar sites were subsequently minimally attended and consequently the 11th Tactical Control Group's Aircraft Control and Warning Squadrons became redundant, all being inactivated on 1 November 1983, except for the 744th ACWS, which moved from Murphy Dome AFS to Elmendorf AFB to man the ROCC. When the Aircraft Control and Warning Squadrons were inactivated the radar sites were re-designated as Long Range Radar (LRR) sites within the Alaska Radar System (ARS).

Although these radar sites were administratively controlled by Alaskan Air Command, they fell under the operational control of NORAD. Likewise, Alaskan Air Command (21st TFW) aircraft conducting air-defence duties were operationally controlled by NORAD. These Alaskan Air Command air-defence units fell specifically under the operational control of the 'Alaskan NORAD Region', the controlled area being identified as the Alaskan Air Defense Sector (AADS).

Another unit that was assigned to the 11th Tactical Control Group was the 3d Air Support Operations Center Flight. It had been activated on 1 June 1980 and assigned directly to Alaskan Air Command. The 3d Air Support Operations Center Flight was reassigned to the 11th Tactical Control Group on 1 July 1981, the day that the latter had been redesignated from 531st Aircraft Control and Warning Group. The 3d Air Support Operations Center Flight trained and deployed FACs and other personnel to operate with US Army units in Alaska. It was redesignated the 3d Air Support Operations Squadron on 6 January 1989.

Commander, Alaskan Air Command was dual-hatted, also serving as Commander, Joint Task Force-Alaska (JTF-AK). JTF-AK was a provisional joint operations unified command that could be activated in the event of war or disasters by the Chairman, Joint Chiefs of Staff; it was responsible for both coordinating the defence of Alaska and coordinating military assistance to civil authorities. Commander, AAC had assumed that dual-hatted responsibility as Commander, JTF-AK after Alaskan Command (ALCOM), a unified command that had existed since 1947, was disestablished in 1975.

The station mascot, an Alaskan Malamute named Pup-Dog, lays in the snow at Kotzebue AFS on 8 March 1982; the radar facilities of the 748th ACWS are visible in the background. (NARA)

Supporters from Stateside

Other USAF MAJCOMs permanently, rotationally or temporarily deployed units and aircraft to the Pacific and Alaska, supporting PACAF, AAC and other agencies.

Strategic Air Command (SAC)

Strategic Air Command's 3d Air Division (3 AD), located at Andersen AFB, Guam, until 12 September 1988 when it moved to Hickam AFB, controlled SAC operations in the Western Pacific, Far East and South East Asia. The 3 AD was directly assigned to SAC headquarters until it was reassigned to SAC's Fifteenth Air Force (15 AF)

A 60th BMS, 43d SW, B-52G Stratofortress dropping Mk 82 SE (Snakeye) retarded 500-lb high-drag bombs at low level over Farallon de Medinilla during exercise Harvest Coconut on 3 December 1984. US forces used the small uninhabited island in the Northern Mariana Islands, 53 miles (85 km) north of Saipan, as a bombing range. The addition of Mk 15 Snakeye retard fin kits to Mk 82 bombs slowed their descent when released, allowing an aircraft dropping at low level to get clear before they impacted below. This B-52 is finished in the 'SIOP Scheme': FS 17875 white undersides and nose (intended to reflect nuclear flash), with FS 34201 tan, FS 34159 medium-green and FS 34079 dark-green upper sides. (NARA)

An 80th TFS F-16B Block 15 escorts a 60th BMS B-52G during an aerial mining mission off Yeosu, South Korea, during Team Spirit '85. Maritime missions were an important part of the 60th BMS's tasking. (NARA)

A year later and another 60th BMS B-52G conducts aerial mining off South Korea during Team Spirit '86. This B-52G is finished in the 'Strategic Camouflage Scheme' which replaced the previous SIOP Scheme on SAC B-52s. It consisted of FS 34086 green drab/FS 36081 dark-grey upper sides and FS 36081 dark-grey/FS 36118 Gunship Gray undersides. (NARA)

on 31 January 1982; its flying components were the 43d Strategic Wing (SW), later redesignated 43d Bombardment Wing (BMW), and the 376th SW.

The 43d SW at Andersen AFB, Guam, was assigned the B-52D-equipped 60th Bombardment Squadron (BMS). One of the last squadrons to operate the B-52D, by 1 October 1983 the 60th BMS replaced them with B-52Gs, deliveries of which had commenced in May (the assigned B-52Gs being former 19th BMW aircraft from Robins AFB). From 1988 onwards the 60th BMS had an exclusively conventional tasking, including Pacific maritime missions. The unit's B-52Gs briefly used fire-breathing dragon markings and later a palm tree. The 43d SW also directly handled TDY KC-135s, until the 65th Strategic Squadron (SS) was activated and assigned to 43d SW on 1 July 1986; thereafter the 65th SS handled tankers and bombers temporarily deployed to Andersen. The TDY KC-135s constituted the Pacific Tanker Task Force (PTTF) and involved SAC, ANG and AFRES KC-135s. On 4 November 1986 43d SW was redesignated 43d BMW.

Andersen AFB itself was reassigned from SAC to PACAF on 1 October 1989, having been assigned to SAC since 1 April 1955.

The 376th SW at Kadena AB, Okinawa, Japan, was assigned 909th Air Refueling Squadron, Heavy (AREFS) with KC-135A/Qs (with 'KADENA' markings). The 376th SW also supported TDY 55th Strategic Reconnaissance Wing (SRW) RC-135s deployed to Kadena from Offutt AFB, Nebraska, and TDY KC-135Qs (usually around six) deployed from the 9th SRW at Beale AFB, California; the KC-135Qs supported SR-71A operations conducted by Det 1, 9th SRW (see below). The 376th SW was assigned to the 3d AD (which was assigned directly to SAC until reassignment to 15th AF on 31 January 1982).

Other SAC flying units in the region, but not administratively assigned to 3d Air Division, were the 6th SW at Eielson AFB and several permanent detachments of the 9th Strategic Reconnaissance Wing (SRW) from Beale AFB.

A 909th AREFS, 376th SW, KC-135A Stratotanker refuels a 35th TFS F-16A Block 10 during Team Spirit '82. Three 44th TFS F-15Cs and another 35th TFS F-16A await their turn. (NARA)

The 6th SW at Eielson AFB was assigned the 24th Strategic Reconnaissance Squadron (SRS). In the early 1980s it operated two RC-135S 'Cobra Ball' Telemetry Intelligence (TELINT) aircraft, which, along with the land-based 'Cobra Dane' radar at Shemya AFB (see below) and the sea-based 'Cobra Judy' radar on board the USNS *Observation Island*, observed Soviet ICBM tests during re-entry and verified Soviet compliance with the Strategic Arms Limitation Treaty (SALT) and other treaties. Consequently, 24th SRS maintained an RC-135S on 24-hour alert at the forward-operating location at Shemya AFB on tiny and remote Shemya in the Aleutian Islands, 1,600 miles (2,575 km) from Eielson and only 500 miles (800 km) from Kamchatka's east coast. Soviet ICBM/SLBM tests would launch from western/central USSR or the Barents Sea/White Sea with their re-entry vehicles targeted at the Klyuchi test range on the Kamchatka Peninsula in the Soviet Far East. At Shemya the alert crew would launch on the sound of the klaxon, being in position off Kamchatka in time to record re-entry with the RC-135S's starboard-side optical sensors. RC-135S 61-2664 was written off while landing in challenging conditions at Shemya on 15 March 1981, tragically killing six crewmen. A replacement RC-135S (converted from C-135B 61-2662) was delivered to 6th SW on 11 November 1983. On 1 April 1988 the 6th SW was redesignated the 6th SRW. A single RC-135X 'Cobra Eye' (62-4128) was delivered to 6th SRW on 16 July 1989, considerably delayed from the originally intended April 1986 delivery due to protracted development. 'Cobra Eye' was designed for midcourse optical tracking and identification of ICBM/SLBM re-entry vehicles via a long-wave infrared telescope. 'Cobra Eye' operated in conjunction with the United States Department of Defense's Strategic Defense Initiative Organization (SDIO) and also supported US ICBM/SLBM tests. The first operational 'Cobra Eye' mission occurred on 15 August 1989. The Cold War's end, the redundancy of its mission and curtailment of SDI projects prematurely ended the operation life of 'Cobra Eye'. It was withdrawn from use and subsequently converted into a third RC-135S in the 1990s. The 24th SRS received one-off RC-135T 55-3121, a former Electronic Intelligence (ELINT) aircraft, on 12 December 1979, for use by 24th SRS as a cockpit trainer for RC-135S crews. In 1982 the RC-135Ts J57-P/F-43Ws were replaced by TF33-PW-102 thrust-reversing turbofans, allowing for more useful training as the RC-135S featured thrust-reversing TF33-P5s (not all TF33 turbofan models featured thrust reversers). NKC-135A

A 28th AREFS, 28th BMW, KC-135A from Ellsworth AFB, South Dakota, is marshalled into a parking position at Andersen AFB in June 1982. It was stopping off at Andersen while deploying from Ellsworth to Darwin, Australia, to participate in exercise Glad Customer '82, along with 28th BMW B-52Hs. (NARA)

Airman Craig D. Barnhart, crew chief with the 5th Organizational Maintenance Squadron (OMS), 5th BMW, signals to a 23d BMS, 5th BMW, B-52H from Minot AFB, North Dakota, on 24 March 1989 while deployed to Eielson during the Strategic Air Command exercise Giant Warrior '89. The near B-52H features the SIOP Scheme modified with the aircraft's white nose overpainted in FS 36081 dark grey to make it less conspicuous at low level, pending a full repaint in the new Strategic Camouflage Scheme seen on the background B-52H. (NARA)

The Osan flight line during Giant Warrior '89. At lower left are a CH-3E (nearest) and a HH-3E of MAC's locally based 38th ARRS. Beyond them is a KC-135A and two B-52Hs, one taxiing, from the 410th BMW, deployed from KI Sawyer AFB, Michigan, for the exercise. In the far background are a USAF C-130 and behind a C-130F of the USN's VRC-50 from NAS Cubi Point in the Philippines. (NARA)

55-3129 was temporarily assigned to 24th SRS as a trainer (3 January–7 April 1982) while the RC-135T was being re-engined. It was originally planned that the RC-135T would be transferred to the 55th SRW at Offutt AFB, Nebraska, as a trainer, after being replaced by dedicated TC-135S trainer 62-4133. However, before the transfer occurred, the RC-135T tragically crashed into a mountain near Valdez Airport, Alaska, while conducting practice approaches on 25 February 1985; all three crewmembers were killed. The TC-135S was delivered to 24th SRS on 22 July 1985.

The 6th SW/SRW also supported TDY RC-135M/V/Ws deployed to Eielson from the 55th SRW and operated Alaskan Tanker Task Force (ATTF) missions with temporary duty (TDY) SAC, ANG and AFRES KC-135s assigned. The wing was assigned to SAC's 47th AD (under 15th AF) and reassigned to 14th AD (also under 15th AF) on 1 October 1985.

The 9th SRW at Beale AFB, California, which was assigned to SAC's 14th AD, maintained several dets in the region. Det 1, 9th SRW at Kadena AB, Okinawa, Japan, operated a pair of SR-71As, reduced to a single SR-71A on 12 August 1988, which finally returned to Beale on 21 January 1990 as Det 1 drew down. Det 2, 9th SRW at Osan AB, South Korea, operated the U-2R. Det 5, 9th SRW at Eielson AFB, operated the SR-71A during the period 1979–80, conducting operational missions and cold-weather tests.

Finally, two notable SAC non-flying units in the region were the 13th Missile Warning Squadron and the 16th Surveillance Squadron, which operated ground-based radar sites within Alaska and the Alaskan Aleutian Islands respectively. SAC had inherited ground-based space-surveillance and missile-warning systems from the inactivating Aerospace Defense Command (ADC) on 1 December 1979, forming SAC's Directorate of Space and Missile Warning Systems. SAC only retained these assets until 1983, when they were transferred to newly activated Space Command.

The 13th Missile Warning Squadron, at Clear AFS, Alaska, operated one of three early warning radar, computer and communications system sites that made up the Ballistic Missile Early Warning System (BMEWS) network. The other two sites were at Thule Site J, near Thule AB, Greenland (operated by the 12th Missile Warning Group, also under SAC), and at RAF Fylingdales, UK (operated by the Royal Air Force).

The 16th Surveillance Squadron at Shemya AFB operated the AN/FPS-108 'Cobra Dane' long-range early warning radar system, used for tracking and gathering intelligence on Soviet ICBM test launches.

Military Airlift Command (MAC)

MAC's airlifter fleet was split between Twenty-First Air Force (21 AF: HQ McGuire AFB, New Jersey), controlling resources east of the Mississippi, and Twenty-Second Air Force (22 AF: HQ Travis AFB, CAlifornia), controlling those to the west. Consequently, 22 AF controlled MAC airlift units stationed in the PACAF and AAC areas of responsibility, apart from Det 1, 89th MAG/MAW (see below), which was under 21 AF.

The 616th Military Airlift Group (MAG) at Elmendorf AFB reported directly to 22 AF. The 616th MAG was directly assigned a couple of operational support airlift C-12Fs; much of their tasking was to support the many remote radar sites across Alaska, which, as outlined above, were originally operated by the Aircraft Control and Warning Squadrons, and which later became Alaska Radar System's Long Range Radar sites. The flying unit assigned to the 616th MAG was the 17th Tactical Airlift

Green Berets of Co. C, 2nd Bn, 7th Special Forces deploy from a 17th TAS, 616th MAG C-130E Hercules while practising for a nocturnal runaway assault during Brim Frost '81. (NARA)

A US Army M973 Small Unit Support Vehicle is offloaded from a 17th TAS, 616th MAG C-130H during Brim Frost '87. The squadron provided 4,000 tons of cargo support during the January 1987 Joint Task Force-Alaska (JTF-AK) exercise. (NARA)

A 20th AAS, 374th TAW, C-9A Nightingale in flight on 22 January 1981. (NARA)

Squadron (TAS) with C-130Es; these were replaced by C-130Hs during 1986. Also assigned to 616th MAG was the 616th Aerial Port Squadron (APS), which was joined by the 16th Mobile Aerial Port Flight from 1 June 1986. Aerial Port Squadrons/ Flights were responsible for all management and movement of cargo and passengers transported in the Military Airlift System. This included processing personnel and cargo, rigging cargoes for airdrop, packing parachutes, loading equipment, preparing air cargo and load plans, loading and securing aircraft, ejecting cargo for inflight delivery, and supervising units engaged in aircraft loading and unloading operations.

The 834th Airlift Division (which was assigned to 22 AF) at Hickam AFB, was responsible for MAC assets in the Pacific and also acted as the airlift adviser for PACAF.

The 374th Tactical Airlift Wing (TAW) at Clark AB, assigned to 834 AD, was the primary MAC airlift organisation in the Pacific. The 374th TAW controlled the 20th Aeromedical Airlift Squadron (AAS), which provided Pacific theatre aeromedical airlift with C-9As and the 21st TAS with C-130Hs.

In order to control the 374th TAW's units in Japan and South Korea, the 316th Tactical Airlift Group (TAG) at Yokota AB had been assigned to the 374th TAW from October 1978 to act as an intermediate tier between the wing headquarters at Clark in the Philippines, and the Japan- and Korea-based units. The 316th TAG controlled the 345th TAS at Yokota which operated C-130Es. The 1403d Military Airlift Squadron (MAS) was activated at Yokota on 1 August 1984 and assigned to 316th TAG, absorbing aircraft from various bases in the Pacific area. The 1403d MAS acted as MAC's operational-support airlift squadron in the Far East, providing intra-theatre airlift for high-ranking PACAF and civilian officials and small mission-essential equipment. Initially, it operated CT-39A OSA aircraft, which it absorbed from the 3d TFW at Clark and the 18th TFW at Kadena as well as from Yokota's 475th ABW. The 1403d MAS activated three detachments on 1 October 1984: Det 1, 1403 MAS at Clark, Det 2, 1403 MAS at Kadena, and Det 3, 1403 MAS at Osan. The dets operated a couple of aircraft each. The 1403d MAS replaced its CT-39As during 1985 with C-21As (stationed at Yokota) and C-12Fs (stationed at the Clark, Kadena and Osan dets). On 1 October 1987 the 13th MAS was activated at Kadena AB and assigned directly to 374th TAW; the 13th MAS replaced Det 2, 1403d MAS and absorbed its

A C-130E of the 345th TAS, 316th TAG, 374th TAW takes off from Osan during Team Spirit '82. It is in the SEA camouflage scheme: FS 34102 medium-green, FS 34079 dark-green and FS 30219 dark-tan upper sides with FS 36622 light-grey undersides. (NARA)

C-12Fs. Dets 1 and 3 of 1403d MAS continued to operate from Clark and Osan for the remainder of the decade.

On 1 October 1989 the 374th TAW, along with its 20th AAS and the 21st TAS components, moved from Clark AB in the Philippines to Yokota AB in Japan. The 37th TAW's intermediate 316th TAG was now superfluous and consequently inactivated at Yokota on the same date; in turn, the 316th TAG's former component units were subsequently reassigned directly to 374th TAW. Henceforth, following the move to Yokota, the 374th TAW directly controlled not only the 20th AAS (C-9As) and the 21st TAS (C-130Hs), but also the 345th TAS (C-130Es) and 1403d MAS (C-21As), all at Yokota, plus the 1403d TAS Dets (C-12Fs) at Clark and Osan and the 13th MAS (C-12Fs) at Kadena.

Military Airlift Support Squadrons (MASS) were support units that had no aircraft of their own; they instead supported the forward operations of aircraft from other MAC units. The MASS was a consolidation of all the operations and maintenance functions that stateside airlift wings had organised as separate units. In the Pacific, the Military Airlift Support Squadrons were assigned to the non-flying 61st Military Airlift Support Wing (MASW), which was stationed at Hickam AFB and assigned to 834th Airlift Division. Assigned Military Airlift Support Squadrons were the 603d MASS at Kadena AB, 605th MASS at Andersen AFB, 607th MASS at Naval Air Facility (NAF) Midway, 611th MASS at Osan AB and the 619th MASS at Hickam AFB. The 61st MASW inactivated on 1 April 1980 with its units being reassigned directly to the 834th Airlift Division. Subsequently, the Military Airlift Support Squadrons at Kadena and Osan were de facto upgraded to Military Airlift Support Group status in 1986; the 603d MASS at Kadena and the 611th MASS at Osan inactivated on 1 January 1986, replaced on the same date by the newly activated 603d MASG at Kadena and 611th MASG at Osan. The inactivated squadrons were subsequently consolidated with the newly activated groups on 3 March 1987, linking their unit heritage and retrospectively creating a common lineage between the inactivated squadrons and their similarly numbered replacement groups. Finally, the 624th MASG was activated at Clark AB on 1 October 1989, which provided support for transient MAC airlifters there following the withdrawal of the 374th TAW from Clark on the same date.

As well as controlling 21 AF and 22 AF, MAC also directly controlled the separate Aerospace Rescue and Recovery Service (HQ: Scott AFB, Illinois). Among the units controlled by the Aerospace Rescue and Recovery Service was the 41st Rescue and Weather Reconnaissance Wing (RWRW) at McClellan AFB, California. The 41st RWRW controlled all active-duty weather reconnaissance squadrons, as well as rescue units in the western United States and the Pacific; in 1980 this included the 33d Aerospace Rescue and Recovery Squadron (ARRS) in the Pacific and the 71st ARRS in Alaska.

The 33d ARRS at Kadena AB provided combat search and rescue (CSAR) support in the Far East, operating as a composite unit with a mixed aircraft fleet consisting of HH-53C rescue helicopters and HC-130H/N/P rescue/tanker aircraft. The HC-130N/P variants could refuel HH-53Cs (and HH-3Es etc.) in-flight while the HC-130H variant could not. The 33d ARRS also maintained two detachments: Det 1 at Clark AB and Det 13 at Osan AB, both flying mixed HH-3E and CH-3E fleets; the HH-3E featured armour protection, air-to-air refuelling capability and other features that the CH-3E lacked.

The 71st ARRS at Elmendorf AFB was also a composite unit, with a mixed HH-3E and HC-130N fleet. Many of the 71st ARRS aircraft featured a unique scheme, adding USAF Arctic markings (consisting of International Orange panels on the nose, tail and

A 33d ARRS, 41st RWRW, HH-53C Super Jolly Green Giant operating from Osan during Team Spirit '82. It is in the SEA camouflage scheme, although both the external fuel tank and the nearest engine cowling have presumably been switched from another HH-53C as they are in the newer 'European I' scheme which substituted Gunship Gray for dark tan. (NARA)

An airman boards a 71st ARRS HH-3E at Eielson, bound for Clear Creek Bare Base, during Brim Frost '81. Like several 71st ARRS HH-3Es, this aircraft features the standard USAF rescue colour scheme (originally used by HC-130s, HH-3s and HH-53s) of overall FS 16473 Light Aircraft Gray with 'RESCUE' title on a black tail stripe and yellow band around the rear fuselage, but modified by the addition of high-visibility USAF Arctic Markings of International Orange on the nose and tail boom. (NARA)

outer wings) to the standard rescue scheme of overall gloss grey with 'RESCUE' title on a black tail stripe and yellow band around the rear fuselage.

Subsequently, there were considerable changes throughout the decade. On 8 January 1981 the 31st ARRS was activated at Clark AB and assigned to 41st RWRW; on the same date the 38th ARRS (previously assigned to the 39th ARRW and stationed at Homestead AFB, Florida) moved without personnel or equipment to Osan AB and was reassigned to the 41st RWRW. The 31st ARRS replaced the former Det 1, 33d ARRS at Clark AB, while the 38th ARRS replaced the former Det 13, 33d ARRS at Osan AB; both those former 33d ARRS dets inactivated on 8 January 1981. The 31st ARRS and 38th ARRS both operated HH-3E and CH-3Es absorbed from the former 33d ARRS dets.

Following Operation Eagle Claw, the disastrous and abortive 1980 attempt to rescue US hostages from Iran, USAF rescue and special operations forces were reorganised. This resulted in the 33d ARRS giving up its HH-53Cs in 1982 to be reassigned to special operation units elsewhere. In exchange the 33d ARRS received less-capable HH-3Es and CH-3Es.

Far more sweeping reorganisation would soon follow in Operation Eagle Claw's wake. This involved the activation of Twenty-Third Air Force (23 AF) at Scott AFB, Illinois, under MAC on 1 March 1983. Twenty-Third Air Force subsequently consolidated the various Special Operations Wings/Squadrons hitherto assigned to

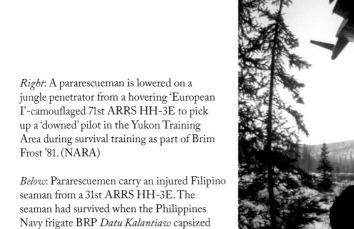

Right: A pararescueman is lowered on a jungle penetrator from a hovering 'European I'-camouflaged 71st ARRS HH-3E to pick up a 'downed' pilot in the Yukon Training Area during survival training as part of Brim Frost '81. (NARA)

Below: Pararescuemen carry an injured Filipino seaman from a 31st ARRS HH-3E. The seaman had survived when the Philippines Navy frigate BRP *Datu Kalantiaw* capsized after being driven aground by Typhoon Clara on 21 September 1981 on the rocky northern shore of Calayan Island, in the northern Philippines, killing seventy-nine of the ninety-seven-man crew. (NARA)

A 31st ARRS CH-3E lands aboard the ammunition ship USS *Mount Hood* (AE-29) off Calayan Island while assisting in salvage operations for the capsized Philippine frigate BRP *Datu Kalantiaw* on 22 September 1981. This SEA-camouflaged CH-3E illustrates the external differences between the CH-3E and HH-3E. Compared with combat SAR HH-3Es, transport CH-3Es lacked the sponson-mounted external fuel tanks, the in-flight refuelling probe and the fixed high-speed rescue hoist (having instead a simple hoist that could be swung in through the door when not in use). The HH-3E also featured crew protection titanium armour and provision for up to three defensive machine guns, which the CH-3E lacked. (NARA)

A 31st ARRS HH-3E delivers Royal New Zealand Air Force VIPs to the Crow Valley Gunnery Range to watch Cope Thunder '84-7 on 10 September 1984. The structure under the central fuselage is a suspension system to support underslung loads. (NARA)

TAC, USAFE and PACAF, plus the various rescue units of the Aerospace Rescue and Recovery Service, as well as other units, under a single MAC Numbered Air Force.

Hitherto assigned directly to MAC headquarters, the Aerospace Rescue and Recovery Service (including its subordinate 41st RWRW) was reassigned to MAC's 23 AF upon the latter's activation on 1 March 1983. However, while the Aerospace Rescue and Recovery Service would remain assigned to 23 AF, on 1 October 1983 the 41st RWRW was reassigned from the Aerospace Rescue and Recovery Service to instead report directly to 23 AF. The 41st RWRW's rescue units also took on an

Medics stretcher a 'casualty' to a 38th ARRS HH-3E during Team Spirit '86. Besides its primary role of rescuing downed aircrew, the 38th ARRS provided logistics support and worked with special operations forces. During summer 1987 the squadron rescued many civilians from floods after Korea was struck by two typhoons. (NARA)

A pararescueman (also known as a 'PJ' due to how they used to be recorded on an Aircrew Flight Log) in front of a 38th ARRS CH-3E while conducting a combat SAR mission during Team Spirit '86. This PJ is armed with a GAU-5A/A rifle (referred to as a 'sub-machine gun' by the USAF), similar to the US Army's XM177E2, itself a carbine version of the M16 rifle. This GAU-5A/A has been retrofitted with a longer 14.5-inch barrel than the 10- or 11.5-inch barrels they were originally delivered with. (NARA)

increasing amount of special operations tasking alongside their previous rescue duties.

During the remainder of the 1980s the 41st RWRW's Pacific and Alaskan-based squadrons developed as follows:

The 31st ARRS, still equipped with HH-3Es/CH-3Es at Clark AB, was redesignated the 31st SOS on 6 April 1989 and was reassigned to the newly activated 353d Special Operations Wing (SOW – see below).

The 33d ARRS retained HH-3Es, CH-3Es and HC-130H/N/Ps at Kadena AB. It was redesignated the 33d Air Rescue Squadron (ARS) on 1 June 1989. On 1 August 1989 the 33d ARS transferred its HC-130s to the newly activated 17th SOS (q.v.) while retaining its CH/HH-3Es. Also on 1 August 1989, the 33d ARS was reassigned from 41st RWRW to instead report directly to the Air Rescue Service. The Aerospace Rescue and Recovery Service had been redesignated the Air Rescue Service (and moved its headquarters from Scott AFB, Illinois, to McClellan AFB, California) on 1 June 1989; the Air Rescue Service remained assigned to MAC's 23 AF.

The 38th ARRS retained its HH-3Es/CH-3Es at Osan AB; it was redesignated the 38th ARS on 1 June 1989 and reassigned from 41st RWRW to the Air Rescue Service on 1 August 1989.

A 33d ARRS HH-3E
Jolly Green Giant at
Kadena on 15 September
1983. F-15s of the
67th TFS are in the
background. (NARA)

A 33d ARRS HH-3E on
15 September 1983. The
Military Airlift Command
version of 'European I'
camouflage, seen here,
consisted of FS 34092
dark green, FS 34102
medium green and FS
36118 Gunship Gray
(i.e. the same two greens
as used by the A-10 etc.,
but with a lighter grey).
(NARA)

Two HH-3Es and
(furthest) a CH-3E of the
33d ARRS over Okinawa
on 14 January 1988.
(NARA)

The 71st ARRS retained its HH-3Es and HC-130Ns at Elmendorf; it was redesignated the 71st ARS on 1 June 1989 and reassigned from 41st RWRW to the Air Rescue Service on 1 August 1989.

With the 41st RWRW's squadrons reassigned out of the wing, the 41st RWRW inactivated on 1 August 1989.

On 1 March 1983, concurrent with the activation of MAC's 23 AF, the 2d Air Division (2 AD) was also activated at Hurlburt Field, Florida, under 23 AF; USAF

A 33d ARRS HC-130P during a 14 January 1988 mission to refuel HH-3Es near Kadena. The HC-130P combined the HC-130H's enlarged radome (barely visible here), and the HC-130N's refuelling tanker capability. All three variants featured an AN/ARD-17 Cook Aerial Tracker in a large fairing atop the forward fuselage; originally introduced to locate manned space capsules during re-entry, it was later used to pick up the locator beacons of downed airmen. (NARA)

special operations units would be consolidated under 2 AD. Consequently, on the same date PACAF's MC-130E-equipped 1st SOS at Clark AB was reassigned from PACAF's 3d TFW to 2d Air Division, Twenty-Third Air Force, MAC. On 1 February 1987 2 AD inactivated and 1st SOS was reassigned directly to 23 AF.

On 6 April 1989 353d SOW was activated at Clark AB and assigned to 23 AF. On the same date MC-130E-equipped 1st SOS and newly redesignated HH-3E-equipped 31st SOS, both located at Clark, were reassigned to 353st SOW. On 1 August 1989 the 17th SOS was activated at Kadena AB and also assigned to 353d SOW; it was equipped with former 33d ARRS HC-130N/Ps.

On 1 October 1987 MAC took over the flight inspection mission (calibrating and evaluating landing approach systems) from Air Force Communications Command (AFCC). Consequently, Det 1, 1467th Facility Checking Squadron (FCS) was activated and took on the role, and the specially equipped T-39A aircraft, of AFCC's former 1868th FCS at Yokota AB (q.v.). Det 1, 1467th FCS was a component of the 375th Aeromedical Airlift Wing (AAW) at Scott AFB, Illinois; the latter was in turn directly assigned to MAC's 23 AF. Exactly a year later, on 1 October 1988, Det 1, 1467th FCS inactivated.

Finally, the 89th MAG, which was redesignated 89th Military Airlift Wing (MAW) on 15 December 1980, at Andrews AFB, Maryland, maintained a permanent detachment at Hickam AFB. The 89th MAG/89th MAW at Andrews was responsible for global Special Air Mission (SAM) support for the president, vice president, combatant commanders and other senior leaders. Meanwhile, Det 1, 89th MAG (which became Det 1, 89th MAW from 15 December 1980) at Hickam operated two C-135C staff transports which provided command support airlift for Commander in Chief, Pacific (CINCPAC) and Commander in Chief, Pacific Air Forces (CINCPACAF). The 89th MAG was assigned to MAC's 76th MAW (also at Andrews and assigned in turn to 21 AF) until 15 December 1980, when the 89th was upgraded to wing status. Thereafter, the 89th MAW was assigned to MAC's 76th Airlift Division (also at Andrews) until being further reassigned directly to 21 AF headquarters on 1 October 1985.

South Korean paratroopers wait to board 463d TAW C-130Es, deployed from Dyess AFB, Texas, to Korea, for an airdrop during Team Spirit '86. (NARA)

A 463d TAW C-130E makes a low-altitude parachute extraction system (LAPES) supply drop at Jo Ju Air Strip during Team Spirit '89. (NARA)

Tactical Air Command (TAC), Air National Guard (ANG) and Air Force Reserve (AFRES)

TAC's 552d Airborne Warning and Control Wing (AWACW) at Tinker AFB, Oklahoma, primarily operated the E-3A Sentry 'AWACS' (Airborne Warning and Control System) aircraft fleet; it was assigned directly to TAC headquarters. As well as the wing's squadrons permanently based at Tinker, the wing also maintained squadrons overseas that handled rotationally forward-deployed E-3s. The 961st Airborne Warning and Control Support Squadron (AWACSS) had been activated at Kadena AB on 1 October 1979 to support and operate rotationally deployed E-3s there. It was redesignated 961st Airborne Warning and Control Squadron (AWACS) on 1 January 1982.

The 552d AWACW's responsibilities later widened and consequently it was redesignated the 552d Airborne Warning and Control Division on 1 October 1983. On 1 April 1985 the 552d reverted to wing status; subsequently the 552d AWACW was assigned to the newly activated 28th Air Division (also at Tinker AFB) which in turn reported directly to TAC. Thirty-four E-3As were ordered by the USAF (although one was retained by Boeing as a test-bed); twenty-four as 'Core E-3As' with AN/APY-1 radar and ten 'Standard E-3As' with AN/APY-2 radar. From the mid-1980s onwards the Core E-3As were upgraded to become E-3Bs, meanwhile those ordered as 'Standard E-3As' actually left the production line as similarly improved E-3Cs.

On 1 July 1986 the 962d AWACS was activated under the 552d at Elmendorf supporting E-3s rotationally deployed there.

Other TAC units periodically deployed from the United States into the PACAF/ AAC regions for exercises.

The state-based reserve units of the Air National Guard naturally included assets in the regions that PACAF and AAC were responsible for through the Alaska ANG and Hawaii ANG.

A plane director signals to a 961st AWACS E-3A Sentry on the Clark flight line during Cope Max '85 while deployed from Kadena on 19 November 1985. This 'Core E-3A', 73-1675 was the fourth E-3A built and the third delivered to the USAF; it was subsequently upgraded to E-3B standard. (NARA)

F-15As of TAC's 94th TFS, 1st TFW, deployed from Langley AFB, Virginia, at Nyutabaru AB, Kyushu, Japan, during Cope North '81-3 in June 1981. Soon afterwards the 1st TFW transitioned from F-15A/Bs to F-15C/Ds. In the foreground is a resident JASDF 202 Hikotai, 5 Kokudan F-104J Starfighter; later that year this squadron reequipped with F-15J/DJs, becoming Japan's first Eagle unit. (NARA)

Left: USAF personnel in cold-weather gear disembark from a SEA-camouflaged C-130E of the 144th TAS, 176th TAG, Alaska ANG, at Kotzebue AFS at the start of Cool Snow Hog '82-1 on 8 March 1982. (NARA)

Below: Technicians prepare live AIM-9Ps and AIM-7Es for an 199th TFS, 154th COMPG, Hawaii ANG, F-4C at Hickam AFB on 21 March 1980. (NARA)

The Alaska ANG controlled the 176th TAG, which was assigned the 144th TAS at Kulis Air National Guard Based (ANGB)/Anchorage International Airport (IAP), with C-130Es, replaced during 1983 with eight new C-130Hs. If called to federal active service ('federalized') by the President, Congress or both, the 144th TAS was gained by MAC. The 176th TAG became 176th Composite Group (COMPG) on 1 October 1986 and was also assigned the SAC-gained 168th AREFS ('ALASKA'/blue) activated at Eielson AFB with four KC-135Es on the same date.

Hawaii ANG's PACAF-gained 154th COMPG controlled 199th TFS 'HANGmen' at Hickam AFB with F-4Cs. The unit was responsible for Hawaiian air defence and also regularly deployed throughout the region to participate in exercises, including to Guam to train with locally based B-52s and exercise the Guam air-defence network, to Misawa AB, Japan, for exercise Cope North, to Clark AB, Philippines, for exercise Cope Thunder and to South Korea for exercise Team Spirit. The 199th TFS converted to the F-15A/B between June 1987 and January 1988. The unit operated Hawaii ANG's operational support airlift aircraft, a C-7A, with a second C-7A being added during the early 1980s; these were replaced by a C-130A in August 1984.

Besides the Alaska- and Hawaii-based ANG units, other ANG units from the lower forty-eight states, as well as units from the federally administered AFRES, regularly conducted TDY deployments into the region, notably KC-135A/E units deploying to support the Alaska Tanker Task Force (ATTF) at Eielson AFB and the Pacific Tanker Task Force (PTTF) at Andersen AFB alongside SAC KC-135A/Rs, as outlined above.

An 199th TFS F-15B escorts a SAC B-1B during exercise Distant Mariner on 13 May 1988. The 96th BMW B-1B was deployed from Dyess AFB, Texas, to Andersen AFB for the exercise. This F-15B, 74-0141, would later be transferred to NASA for use as an Aeronautics Research Testbed. (NARA)

Left: Oregon Air National Guard personnel, of the 104th Tactical Control Flight (Forward Air Control Post), 154th Tactical Control Group, set up a TPS-43E radar antenna and control vans at Pedro Dome, Alaska, on 15 January 1983 during Brim Frost '83. The 104th TCF (FACP) was deployed from North Bend ANG Station near Hauser, Oregon. (NARA)

Below: Personnel of the California ANG's 146th Aeromedical Evacuation Squadron transfer 'patients' from a C-130H of the 158th TAS, 165th TAG, Georgia ANG to an ambulance at Kimhae in March 1984 during Team Spirit '84. The 'European I' camouflaged Georgia ANG C-130H was deployed from its base at Savannah Municipal Airport. A SEA camouflaged C-130H in the background is from 183d TAS, 172d TAG, Mississippi ANG, based at Jackson Municipal Airport (Allen C. Thompson Field). (NARA)

Air Force Communications Command (AFCC)

AFCC's 1867th FCS conducted the flight inspection mission from Yokota AB, operating a specially equipped T-39A. The 1867th FCS was assigned to AFCC's Pacific Communications Area, which was repeatedly redesignated throughout the decade, becoming Pacific Communications Division on 1 June 1981 and Pacific Information Systems Division on 15 August 1984 before reverting to Pacific Communications Division on 1 November 1986.

As outlined above, on 1 October 1987 MAC took over the flight inspection mission from AFCC; 1867th FCS moved without personnel or equipment to Scott AFB, was redesignated 1467th FCS and absorbed the inactivating 1866th FCS (based at Scott AFB) and 1868th FCS (based at Rhein-Main) and was reassigned to MAC. The former 1867th FCS aircraft and other assets at Yokota were absorbed by the new Det 1, 1467th FCS under MAC.

Electronic Security Command (ESC)

ESC was headquartered at Kelly AFB, Texas, and had been known as the United States Air Force Security Service (USAFSS) until being redesignated on 1 August 1979. ESC monitored, collected and interpreted the military voice and electronic signals of countries of interest.

During 1980, most of ESC's units in Alaska and the Pacific, which had hitherto been assigned directly to ESC headquarters, were reassigned to ESC's 'Headquarters, Electronic Security, Pacific' (ESP), headquartered at Hickam AFB. On 1 October 1983 'Headquarters, Electronic Security, Alaska' (ESA) was activated at Elmendorf AFB, absorbing ESC's Alaskan-based units. On 1 October 1986 'Headquarters, Electronic Security, Pacific' was redesignated as an ESC Division, becoming 'HQ Pacific Electronic Security Division' (PESD).

The 6903d Electronic Security Squadron (ESS) at Osan AB supported SAC's Det 2, 9th SRW U-2 operations at the base. It was redesignated the 6903d Electronic Security Group (ESG) on 1 October 1981. It was assigned directly to ESC headquarters, until being reassigned to ESP on 30 September 1980, the latter becoming PESD on 1 October 1986.

The 6920th ESG at Misawa AB operated a distinctive AN/FLR-9 Wullenweber 'Elephant Cage' high-frequency direction-finding antenna array, which was part of a worldwide 'Iron Horse' network of such arrays. It was reassigned from ESC headquarters to ESP on 30 September 1980, the latter becoming PESD on 1 October 1986.

The 6922d ESS at Clark AB also operated an AN/FLR-9 'Elephant Cage'. It was reassigned from ESC headquarters to ESP on 30 September 1980, the latter becoming PESD on 1 October 1986.

The 6924th ESS at Wheeler AFB was activated on 1 August 1980 and provided intelligence support in Hawaii. It was assigned to ESP, the latter becoming PESD on 1 October 1986. The 6924th ESS was redesignated the 6924th ESG on 1 August 1986.

The 6981st ESS at Elmendorf AFB operated an AN/FLR-9 'Elephant Cage'; it was redesignated 6981st ESG on 1 April 1989. It was reassigned from ESC to ESP on 15 May 1980, then ESA upon the latter's activation on 1 October 1983. On 1 June 1989 6981st ESG was reassigned back to PSED.

The 6985th ESS at Eielson AFB provided the on-board intelligence specialists which joined the SAC crews aboard the 6th SW/SRW RC-135s. They not only supported operations of the 6th SW/SRW's assigned RC-135S 'Cobra Ball' TELINT aircraft, but also the RC-135V/W Rivet Joint ELINT aircraft on TDY deployments to the 6th SW/SRW at Eielson from SAC's 55th SRW at Offutt AFB, Nebraska. The 6985th ESS was assigned directly to ESC's 'Headquarters, Electronic Security, Strategic' (ESS) at Offutt AFB, until being reassigned to ESA upon the latter's activation on 1 October 1983.

The 6990th ESS at Kadena AB, which was redesignated the 6990th ESG on 1 May 1980, supported 55th SRW RC-135V/W Rivet Joints on TDY deployments to Kadena, providing cryptologic linguist aircrew, airborne special signals operators, airborne maintenance specialists and information integration officers during operational reconnaissance missions. The 6990th ESS/ESG also supported 961st AWACSS/AWACS E-3 operations. The 6990th ESS/ESG was assigned directly to ESC until being reassigned to ESP on 1 May 1980, the latter becoming PESD on 1 October 1986.

Two 432d TFW F-16A Block 15s fly over the 6920th ESG's facilities at Misawa during 1985, including the distinctive AN/FLR-9 Wullenweber 'Elephant Cage' high-frequency direction-finding antenna array. (NARA)

End of an Era

The rapid conclusion of the Cold War during the period 1989–91 soon resulted in major defence cuts. The USAF, already facing funding cuts in 1989, would endure further reductions during the 1990s.

However, while the threat faced by USAFE in Europe had almost entirely evaporated, and that command consequently saw huge force reductions, many of the threats faced in the Asia-Pacific remained. Therefore, PACAF retained most of its strength beyond the 1980s. Wider restructuring, both locally and more generally across the USAF, would have more impact on PACAF and AAC, starting with the inactivation of AAC, and its absorption by PACAF.

As noted above, the Commander, Alaskan Air Command was dual-hatted, also serving as Commander, Joint Task Force-Alaska (JTF-AK), a provisional joint unified command that was only activated in an emergency. The *Exxon Valdez* oil spill in March 1989 resulted in the emergency activation of JTF-AK. However, JTF-AK could not adequately supply the resources required for this scale of operation. Consequently, Alaskan Command (ALCOM) was re-established during 1989 (having previously been disestablished in 1975); this permanently placed all military forces in Alaska under the leadership of a single commander, resolving the previously disjointed command.

As a consequence of these changes, it was subsequently decided to place AAC, which was now Alaskan Command's air component, under PACAF. Therefore, on 9 August 1990 Alaskan Air Command changed status from a MAJCOM to a Numbered Air Force, being redesignated as the Eleventh Air Force (11 AF) and reassigned to PACAF.

The negotiations between the US and Philippine governments to extend the lease of Clark AB and other US military facilities in the Philippines were at an impasse. Any hopes of a resolution were stymied by the eruption of Mount Pinatubo in June 1991, which caused considerable damage to Clark AB and forced its closure. US military personnel and their families were evacuated from Clark AB and US Naval Base Subic Bay in Operation Fiery Vigil. The USAF transferred Clark AB to the Philippine government in November 1991, ending based USAF operations within the Philippines.

Effective from 2 December 1991, Thirteenth Air Force was relocated from Clark AB to Andersen AFB, Guam, where it became responsible both for non-flying units there and also a newly established non-flying presence at Paya Lebar AB in Singapore, which supported training deployments of USAF combat aircraft to the Republic of Singapore Air Force base.

The USAF was completely reorganised in 1992 as a result of the lessons learned during the Gulf War (Operations Desert Shield/Storm, 1990–91, which included the deployment of 3d TFW F-4Es to Turkey to provide Pave Tack LGB guidance support for other Turkish-based USAF combat aircraft attacking Iraq from the north).

SAC, TAC and MAC were all inactivated, replaced by two new MAJCOMs, Air Combat Command (ACC) and Air Mobility Command (AMC), which divided the assets of the three inactivated MAJCOMs. As part of this restructure, PACAF directly absorbed the various supporting assets previously provided by deployments from SAC, TAC and MAC, including the C-9As, C-130s, E-3s and KC-135s. PACAF would also subsequently be the gaining command for any federalised Alaska or Hawaii ANG units.

As part of the restructuring of the USAF in the early 1990s, which also saw a draw-down of the force in the post-Cold War period, a number of units were effectively redesignated in order to preserve the heritage of historically significant units that were being inactivated. For example, the 432d TFW at Misawa AB, which had been redesignated the 432d Fighter Wing (FW) on 31 May 1991 as part of the USAF restructure, was inactivated on 1 October 1994; in its place the historically notable 35th FW was activated on the same date, absorbing the component units and assets of the former 432d FW.

Bibliography

Anderegg, C. R., *Sierra Hotel - Flying Air Force Fighters in the Decade After Vietnam* (Washington, DC: Air Force History and Museums Program, United States Air Force, 2001)

Bell, Dana, *USAF Colors and Markings in the 1990s* (London: Lionel Leventhal Limited, 1992)

Crickmore, Paul F., *Lockheed SR-71 Operations in the Far East* (Oxford: Osprey Publishing, 2008)

Davies, Steve and Dildy, Doug, *F-15 Eagle Engaged: The World's Most Successful Jet Fighter* (Oxford: Osprey Publishing, 2007)

Donald, David (ed.), *US Air Force Air Power Directory* (London: Aerospace Publishing Limited, 1992)

Francillon, René J., *The United States Air National Guard* (London: Aerospace Publishing Limited, 1993)

Hopkins III, Robert S., *The Boeing KC-135 Stratotanker* (Manchester: Crécy Publishing Limited, 2018)

Lake, Jon (ed.), *McDonnell F-4 Phantom: Spirit in the Sky* (London: Aerospace Publishing Limited, 1992)

Martin, Patrick, *Tail Code: The Complete History of USAF Tactical Aircraft Tail Code Markings* (Atglen: Schiffer Publishing Limited, 1994)

Peake, William R., *McDonnell Douglas F-4 Phantom II Production and Operational Data* (Hinckley: Midland Publishing, 2004)

Roberts, Michael, *The Illustrated Directory of the United States Air Force* (London: Brian Trodd Publishing House Limited)

Rogers, Brian, *United States Air Force Unit Designations since 1978* (Hinckley: Midland Publishing, 2005)

Symonds, Adrian, *ANG in the 1980s* (Stroud: Amberley Publishing Limited, 2022)

Symonds, Adrian, *SAC in the 1980s* (Stroud: Amberley Publishing Limited, 2022)

Symonds, Adrian, *TAC in the 1980s* (Stroud: Amberley Publishing Limited, 2021)

Symonds, Adrian, *US Naval Aviation in the 1980s: Air Stations of the Atlantic and Pacific Fleets* (Stroud: Amberley Publishing Limited, 2023)

Symonds, Adrian, *USAFE in the 1980s* (Stroud: Amberley Publishing Limited, 2020)

Thigpen, Jerry, *The Praetorian STARShip: The Untold Story of the Combat Talon* (Maxwell AFB, Alabama: Air University Press, 2001)

Thornborough, Anthony M., *USAF Phantoms – Tactics, Training and Weapons* (London: Arms & Armour Press, 1988)

Thornborough, Anthony M. and Davies, Peter E., *The Phantom Story* (London: Arms & Armour Press, 1994)
Williamson, Justin W., *Operation Eagle Claw 1980* (Oxford: Osprey Publishing, 2020)

Journals and Periodicals

United States Air Force Yearbook, various annual editions (Royal Air Force Benevolent Fund's International Air Tattoo Publishing Unit)
World Air Power Journal, various volumes (Aerospace Publishing Limited)

Appendix I

Structure January 1980

Pacific Air Forces

HQ: Hickam AFB, Hawaii

Direct Reporting

15th ABW (Hickam AFB, Hawaii)
(Directly assigned T-33As for Hawaii adversary/target support.)
9th ACCS – EC-135J
22d TASS – O-2A (blue fin cap) (Geographically separated unit at Wheeler AFB, Hawaii; 22d TASS was reassigned to 326th AD on 4 April 1980.)

326th Air Division (**Wheeler AFB, Hawaii**)
(326th AD coordinated Hawaii's air defences via the 6010th and 6491st Aerospace Defense Flights.)

Fifth Air Force, Yokota AB, Japan

475th ABW (Yokota AB, Japan – host unit supporting MAC's resident 316th TAG)
(Directly assigned CT-39A operational support airlift aircraft, and UH-1Ps. The UH-1Ps were replaced with UH-1Ns during 1980.)

313th Air Division (**Kadena AB, Okinawa**)

18th TFW (Kadena AB, Okinawa, 'ZZ')
(Directly assigned CT-39A operational support airlift aircraft.)
18th TFG
1st SOS – MC-130E (no tail code or squadron colour)
12th TFS – F-4D (yellow)
15th TRS – RF-4C (black/yellow checkerboard)
25th TFS – F-4D (green)
44th TFS – F-15C/D (black)
67th TFS – F-15C/D (red)
Det 1, 18th TFW – F-15C/D, RF-4C (Osan AB, South Korea) (Under 314th Air Division operational control.)

314th Air Division (Osan AB, South Korea)

8th TFW (Kunsan AB, South Korea, 'WP')
35th TFS – F-4D (blue)
80th TFS – F-4D (yellow)
497th TFS - F-4D (red) (Geographically separated unit at Taegu AB, South Korea.)

51st COMPW (Osan AB, South Korea, 'OS')
36th TFS – F-4E (red)
19th TASS - OV-10A (no squadron colour)
(**5th TAIRCG** activated on 8 January 1980, assigned to 51st COMPW and subsequently
   controlling 19th TASS)

Thirteenth Air Force, Clark AB, Luzon, Philippines

3d TFW (Clark AB, Philippines, 'PN')
(Directly assigned T-33As for Cope Thunder adversary/target support, and CT-39A
   operational support airlift aircraft.)
3d TFS – F-4E (blue)
26th TFTAS – F-5E, T-38A (no tail code or squadron colour)
90th TFS – F-4E/G (red)

6200th TFTG (Clark AB, Philippines)
1st TESTS - BQM-34A (plus F-4Es borrowed from 3rd TFW)

Alaskan Air Command

HQ: Elmendorf AFB, Alaska

21st TFW (Elmendorf AFB, Alaska, 'FC')
(Directly assigned T-33As for Alaska adversary/target support, and a C-12A.)
18th TFS – F-4E (blue)
43d TFS – F-4E (gold)
5071st ABS (Non-flying host unit at King Salmon AFS.)
5072d ABS (Non-flying host unit at Galena AFS.)

5010 CSG (Eielson AFB, Alaska) (Directly assigned T-33As.)
25th TASS – O-2A

531st ACWG (Elmendorf AFB, Alaska) (Controlled Aircraft Control and Warning Squadrons
   operating manned surveillance radar and Ground Control Intercept radar sites.)
705th ACWS (King Salmon AFS)
708th ACWS (Indian Mountain AFS)
710th ACWS (Tin City AFS)
711th ACWS (Cape Lisburne AFS)

714th ACWS (Cold Bay AFS)
717th ACWS (Tatalina AFS)
719th ACWS (Sparrevohn AFS)
743d ACWS (Campion AFS)
744th ACWS (Murphy Dome AFS)
748th ACWS (Kotzebue AFS)
794th ACWS (Cape Newenham AFS)
795th ACWS (Cape Romanzof AFS)

Strategic Air Command

Alaska- and Pacific-based units:

Direct Reporting to SAC HQ

3d Air Division (Andersen AFB, Guam)
43d SW (Andersen AFB, Guam)
60th BMS – B-52D
(43d SW also controlled TDY SAC/ANG/AFRES KC-135s (constituting the Pacific
  Tanker Task Force).)

376th SW (Kadena AB, Okinawa, Japan)
909th AREFS – KC-135A/Q
(376th SW also controlled TDY KC-135Qs and RC-135M/V/Us.)

Fifteenth Air Force, March AFB, California

14th Air Division (Beale AFB, California)

9th SRW (Beale AFB, California)
Det 1, 9th SRW – SR-71A (Kadena AB, Okinawa, Japan)
Det 2, 9th SRW – U-2R (Osan AB, South Korea)
Det 5, 9th SRW – SR-71A (Eielson AFB, Alaska)

47th Air Division (Fairchild AFB, Washington)

6th SW (Eielson AFB, Alaska)
24th SRS – RC-135S/T
(6th SW also controlled TDY KC-135s and RC-135M/V/Us.)

Military Airlift Command

Alaska- and Pacific-based units:

Twenty-First Air Force, McGuire AFB, New Jersey

76th MAW (Andrews AFB, Maryland)
89th MAG (Andrews AFB, Maryland)
Det 1, 89th MAG – C-135C (Hickam AFB, Hawaii) (Command support airlift for CINCPAC and CINCPACAF.)

Twenty-Second Air Force, HQ Travis AFB, California

616th MAG (Elmendorf AFB, Alaska)
(Directly assigned C-12F operational support airlift aircraft.)
17th TAS – C-130E

834th Airlift Division (Hickam AFB, Hawaii)

374th TAW (Clark AB, Philippines)
20th AAS – C-9A
21st TAS – C-130H
316th TAG (Yokota AB, Japan) (Directly assigned to 374th TAW).
345th TAS – C-130E

Aerospace Rescue and Recovery Service, Scott AFB, Illinois

41st RWRW (McClellan AFB, California)
33d ARRS – HH-53C, HC-130H/N/P (Kadena AB, Okinawa, Japan)
Det 1, 33d ARRS – HH-3E, CH-3E (Clark AB, Philippines)
Det 13, 33d ARRS – HH-3E, CH-3E (Osan AB, South Korea)
71st ARRS – HH-3E, HC-130N (Elmendorf AFB, Alaska)

Tactical Air Command

Pacific-based unit:

552d AWACW (Tinker AFB, Oklahoma)
961st AWACSS – TDY E-3As (Kadena AB, Okinawa, Japan)

Alaska Air National Guard

176th TAG (Kulis ANGB/Anchorage IAP)
144th TAS – C-130E (Gained by MAC if federalised.)

Hawaii Air National Guard

154th COMPG (Hickam AFB, Hawaii)
199th TFS – F-4C, plus C-7A operational support airlift aircraft (Gained by PACAF if federalised; responsible for Hawaiian air defence.)

Air Force Communications Command (AFCC)

Pacific-based unit:

Pacific Communications Area

1867th FCS – T-39A (Yokota AB, Japan) (Flight inspection.)

Appendix II

Structure January 1989

Pacific Air Forces

HQ: Hickam AFB, Hawaii

Direct Reporting

15th Air Base Wing (Hickam AFB, Hawaii)
9th ACCS – EC-135J

326th Air Division (Wheeler AFB, Hawaii)

(326th AD coordinated Hawaii's air defences via the 6010th and 6491st Aerospace Defense Flights.)

Fifth Air Force, Yokota AB, Japan

432d TFW (Misawa AB, Japan, 'MJ')
13th TFS – F-16C/D Block 30 (black/white checkerboard)
14th TFS – F-16C/D Block 30 (black/yellow checkerboard)

475th ABW (Yokota AB, Japan – host unit supporting MAC's resident 374th TAW)
(Directly assigned support UH-1Ns.)

313th Air Division (Kadena AB, Okinawa)

18th TFW (Kadena AB, Okinawa, 'ZZ')
12th TFS – F-15C/D (yellow)
15th TRS – RF-4C (black/yellow checkerboard) (Reassigned to 460th TRG and moved
    to Taegu AB, South Korea, under 7 AF on 1 October 1989.)
26th AS – non-operational/no aircraft; awaiting F-16C Block 30
44th TFS – F-15C/D (black)
67th TFS – F-15C/D (red)
Det 1, 18th TFW – F-15C/D, RF-4C (Osan AB, South Korea) (Under Seventh Air Force
    operational control.)

Seventh Air Force, Osan AB, South Korea

8th TFW (Kunsan AB, South Korea, 'WP')
35th TFS – F-16C/D Block 30 (blue)
80th TFS – F-16C/D Block 30 (yellow)

51st TFW (Osan AB, South Korea, 'OS')
25th TFS – A-10A (green, 'SU') (Suwon AB, South Korea.)
36th TFS – F-4E (red) (Transitioned to F-16C/D Block 30 between January and
    June 1989.)
497th TFS – F-4E (blue, 'GU') (Taegu AB, South Korea.)

5th TAIRCG (Osan AB, South Korea, 'OS')
19th TASS – OV-10A (blue)
(5th TAIRCG and 19th TASS moved to Suwon AB, South Korea on 1 August 1989,
    transitioning to OA-10As ('SU'/blue).)

Thirteenth Air Force, Clark AB, Luzon, Philippines

3d TFW (Clark AB, Philippines, 'PN')
(Directly assigned UH-1Ns for Cope Thunder support.)
3d TFS – F-4E (blue)
90th TFS – F-4E/G (red)

6200th TFTG (Clark AB, Philippines)
1st TESTS – BQM-34A (plus F-4Es borrowed from 3rd TFW) (BQM-34As replaced
    by MQM-107s during 1989.)

Alaskan Air Command

HQ: Elmendorf AFB, Alaska

21st TFW (Elmendorf AFB, Alaska, 'AK')
43d TFS – F-15C/D (blue)
54th TFS – F-15C/D (yellow)
5071st ABS (Non-flying host unit at King Salmon AFS.)
5072d ABS (Non-flying host unit at Galena AFS.)

343d TFW (Eielson AFB, Alaska, 'AK')
18th TFS – A-10A (blue)
25th TASS – OV-10A (red)

11th TCG (Elmendorf AFB, Alaska)
744th ACWS (Manned the Elmendorf Region Operations Control Center.)

Strategic Air Command

Alaska- and Pacific-based units:

Fifteenth Air Force, March AFB, California

3d Air Division (Hickam AFB, Hawaii)

43d BMW (Andersen AFB, Guam)
60th BMS – B-52G
65th SS – TDY SAC/ANG/AFRES KC-135s (constituting the Pacific Tanker Task
  Force) and TDY SAC bombers

376th SW (Kadena AB, Okinawa, Japan)
909th AREFS – KC-135A/Q
(376th SW also controlled TDY KC-135Qs and TDY RC-135R/V/Us.)

14th Air Division (Beale AFB, California)

6th SRW (Eielson AFB, Alaska)
24th SRS – RC-135S/TC-135S (Joined by an RC-135X from July 1989.)
(6th SW also controlled TDY KC-135s and RC-135R/V/Us.)

9th SRW (Beale AFB, California)
Det 1, 9th SRW – SR-71A (Kadena AB, Okinawa, Japan)
Det 2, 9th SRW – U-2R (Osan AB, South Korea)

Military Airlift Command

Alaska- and Pacific-based units:

Twenty-First Air Force, McGuire AFB, New Jersey

89th MAW (Andrews AFB, Maryland)
Det 1, 89th MAW – C-135C (Hickam AFB, Hawaii) (Command support airlift for
CINCPAC and CINCPACAF.)

Twenty-Second Air Force, HQ Travis AFB, California

616th MAG (Elmendorf AFB, Alaska)
(Directly assigned C-12F operational support airlift aircraft.)
17th TAS – C-130H

834th Airlift Division (Hickam AFB, Hawaii)

374th TAW (Clark AB, Philippines)
20th AAS – C-9A
21st TAS – C-130H
316th TAG (Yokota AB, Japan) (Directly assigned to 374th TAW.)
345th TAS – C-130E
1403d MAS – C-21A
Det 1, 1403 MAS – C-12F (Clark AB, Philippines)
Det 3, 1403 MAS – C-12F (Osan AB, South Korea)
13th MAS – C-12F (Kadena AB, Okinawa, Japan)
(On 1 October 1989 the 374th TAW, and its 20th AAS and 21st TAS components, moved from Clark AB in the Philippines to Yokota AB in Japan and the intermediate 316th TAG was inactivated.)

Twenty-Third Air Force, Scott AFB, Illinois

1st SOS – MC-130E (Clark AB, Philippines) (Directly assigned to 23 AF; reassigned to newly activated 353d SOW on 6 April 1989.)

41st RWRW (McClellan AFB, California) (41st RWRW inactivated on 1 August 1989.)
31st ARRS – HH-3E, CH-3E (Clark AB, Philippines) (Redesignated 31st SOS on 6 April 1989 and reassigned to newly activated 353d SOW.)
33d ARRS – HH-3E, CH-3E, HC-130H/N/P (Kadena AB, Okinawa, Japan) (Redesignated 33d ARS on 1 June 1989. On 1 August 1989 the 33d ARS transferred its HC-130s to newly activated 17th SOS, 353d SOW, while retaining its HH-3Es, and was reassigned to report directly to the Air Rescue Service.)
38th ARRS – HH-3E, CH-3E (Osan AB, South Korea) (Redesignated 38th ARS on 1 June 1989 and reassigned to report directly to the Air Rescue Service on 1 August 1989.)
71st ARRS – HH-3E, HC-130N (Elmendorf AFB, Alaska) (Redesignated 71st ARS on 1 June 1989 and reassigned to report directly to the Air Rescue Service on 1 August 1989.)

Tactical Air Command

Alaska- and Pacific-based units:

28th Air Division (Tinker AFB, Oklahoma)

552d AWACW (Tinker AFB, Oklahoma)
961st AWACS – TDY E-3B/Cs (Kadena AB, Okinawa, Japan)
962d AWACS – TDY E-3B/Cs (Elmendorf AFB, Alaska)

Alaska Air National Guard

176th COMPG (Kulis ANGB/Anchorage IAP)
144th TAS – C-130H (Gained by MAC if federalised.)
168th AREFS – KC-135E (Eielson AFB) (Gained by SAC if federalised.)

Hawaii Air National Guard

154th COMPG (Hickam AFB, Hawaii)
199th TFS – F-15A/B plus C-130A operational support airlift aircraft (Gained by PACAF if federalised; responsible for Hawaiian air defence.)